TEACHER APPROVED

GET READY FOR
KINDERGARTEN

584 ACTIVITIES & **3,825** ILLUSTRATIONS

BLACK DOG
& LEVENTHAL
PUBLISHERS

TEACHER APPROVED

GET READY FOR
KINDERGARTEN

HEATHER STELLA

584 ACTIVITIES & **3,825** ILLUSTRATIONS

BLACK DOG
& LEVENTHAL
PUBLISHERS

Black Dog & Leventhal Publishers
Hachette Book Group
1290 Avenue of the Americas
New York, NY 10104
www.hachettebookgroup.com
www.blackdogandleventhal.com

Printed in China

Cover and interior design by Marlyn Dantes

APS

First Edition: May 2016

10 9 8 7 6

Black Dog & Leventhal Publishers is an imprint of Hachette Books, a division of Hachette Book Group.
The Black Dog & Leventhal Publishers name and logo are trademarks of Hachette Book Group, Inc.
The Hachette Speakers Bureau provides a wide range of authors for speaking events. To find out more, go to www.HachetteSpeakersBureau. com or call (866) 376-6591.
The publisher is not responsible for websites (or their content) that are not owned by the publisher.

ISBN 978-0-316-35225-3

CONTENTS

7   **A NOTE TO PARENTS**

9   **ALPHABET**

87   **SIGHT WORDS**

130   **SIZES, COMPARISONS, & OPPOSITES**

171   **NUMBERS & COUNTING**

213   **COLORS & SHAPES**

239   **TIME & DATE**

260   **ME & MY WORLD**

280   **NATURE & SCIENCE**

306   **SUGGESTED READING**

307   **ANSWER KEY**

A NOTE TO PARENTS

GET READY FOR KINDERGARTEN is an indispensable educational companion for your pre-kindergarten child. It is chock-full of fun, interesting, curriculum-based activities—such as those focusing on the alphabet, numbers, colors, shapes, math readiness, nature, and more—that will introduce your child to new concepts while reinforcing what he or she already knows. In addition, there are plenty of fun word games, mazes, and coloring activities that are designed to entertain and amuse your child while boosting his or her basic skills.

In the back of the book you will find a Suggested Reading list. We recommend setting aside some time each day to read with your child. The more your child reads,

the faster he or she will acquire other skills. We also suggest that you have your child complete a portion of the book each day. You and your child can sit down and discuss what the goals for each day will be, and perhaps even choose a reward to be given upon completion of the whole book—such as a trip to the park, a special playdate, or something else that seems appropriate to you. While you want to help your child set educational goals, be sure to offer lots of encouragement along the way. These activities are not meant as a test. By making them fun and rewarding, you will help your child look forward to completing them, and he or she will be especially eager to tackle the educational challenges ahead!

Hey, kids!
Remember to have
a pencil and
some crayons
handy when
playing with your
Get Ready book!

ALPHABET

Uppercase Letter A

A is for _____**PPLE**. 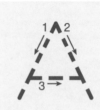 Trace the uppercase letter **A**.
Then try writing it on your own.

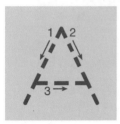 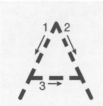 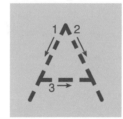 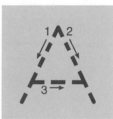

start

Help the **A**lligator get to the water by following
the path of uppercase letter **A**.

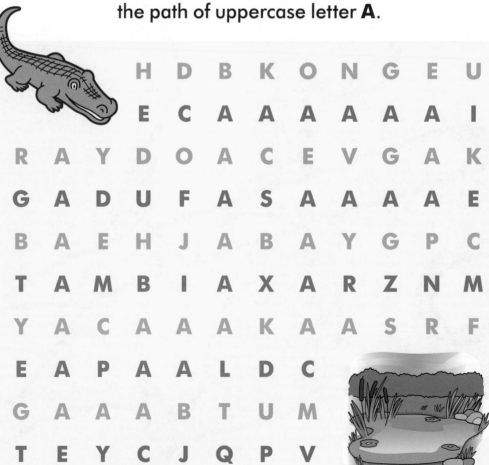

H D B K O N G E U
E C A A A A A A I
R A Y D O A C E V G A K
G A D U F A S A A A A E
B A E H J A B A Y G P C
T A M B I A X A R Z N M
Y A C A A A K A A S R F
E A P A A L D C
G A A A B T U M
T E Y C J Q P V

Lowercase Letter a

Trace the lowercase letter **a**.
Then try writing it on your own.

start

Write the beginning letter **a** to complete the words.

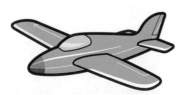 ___nt

 ___pple

 ___corn

 ___irplane

Beginning Sounds

Ant 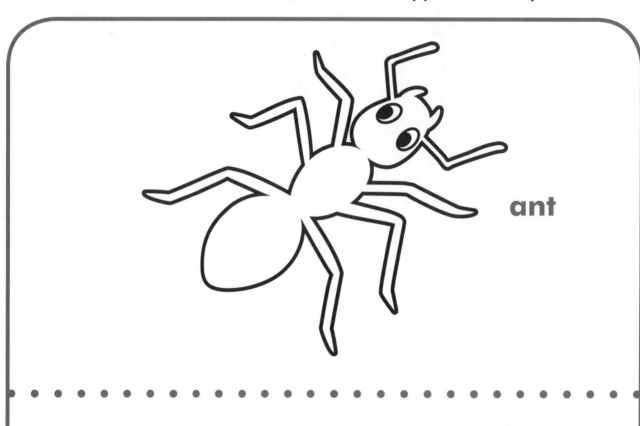 begins with the letter **A**.
Color the **A**nt. Then draw your own picture of something
that starts with the letter **A**, such as an **a**pple or an **a**irplane.

ant

Uppercase Letter B

B is for _____EAR.  Trace the uppercase letter **B**.
Then try writing it on your own.

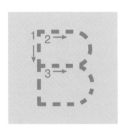   

start

B is for **BUTTERFLY**. Circle the letter **B**'s within the outlines.
Color the picture to make your own **BUTTERFLY**.

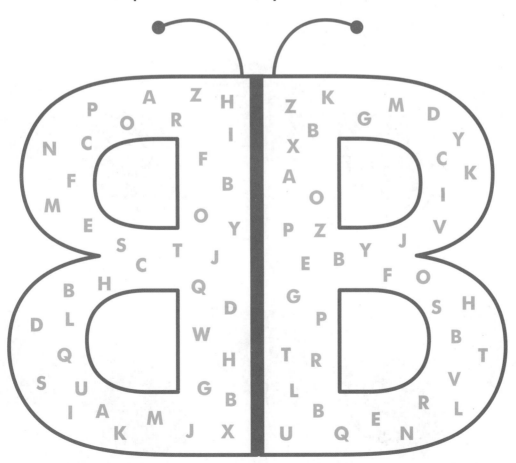

13

Lowercase Letter b

Trace the lowercase letter **b**.
Then try writing it on your own.

start

B is for **b**ird. Draw a line from the uppercase
letter **B**'s to the lowercase letter **b**'s.

B   F   P   B   B

d   b   b   r   b

Beginning Sounds

Circle the picture that has the same beginning sound as the first one.

boat

sun

carrot

deer

car

bed

Uppercase Letter C

C is for _____AR.  Trace the uppercase letter **C**.
Then try writing it on your own.

start
•

C is for **COW**. Color the letter **C**.
Color the **COW**.

Lowercase Letter c

Trace the lowercase letter **c**.
Then try writing it on your own.

start

C is for **CIRCLE**. Find your way to the
center of this **c**ircle maze.

Beginning Sounds

Say the word **c**at. Cat starts with the **C** sound.
Color any pictures below that begin with the **C** sound.

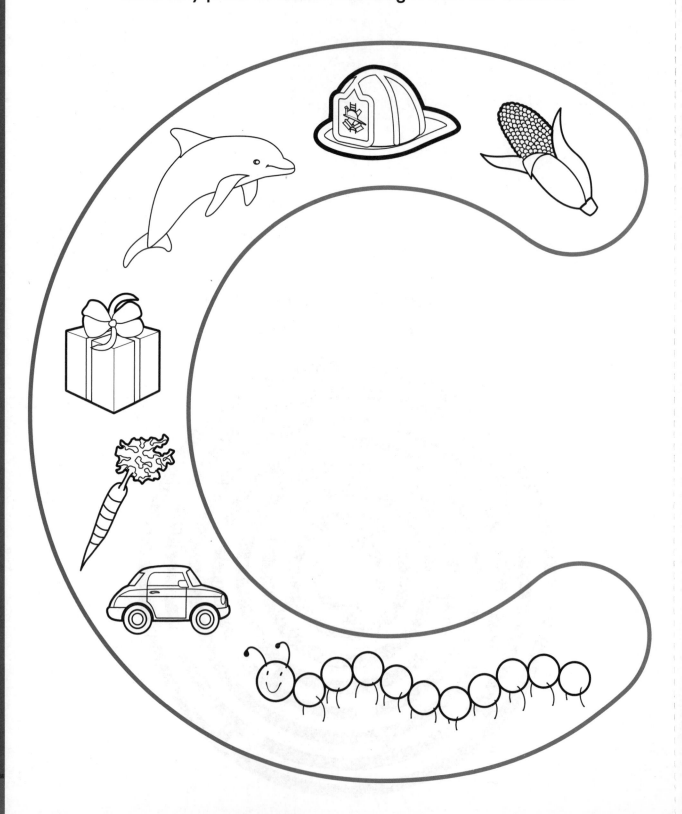

Uppercase Letter D

D is for _____**UCK**.  Trace the uppercase letter **D**. Then try writing it on your own.

start

Fill in the missing **D** to complete the words.

 **D** is for _____OG

 D is for _____OLL

 **D** is for _____INOSAUR

 D is for _____OUGHNUT

Lowercase Letter d

Trace the lowercase letter **d**.
Then try writing it on your own.

start

Draw a line from each of the uppercase **D**'s on the **d**ucks to
one of the lowercase **d**'s on the **d**ucklings below.

Beginning Sounds

Say the word **dog**. **Dog** starts with the **D** sound.
Say the name of each picture. Circle all of the
pictures that begin with the **D** sound.

D

Uppercase Letter E

E is for _____GGS.  Trace the uppercase letter **E**.
Then try writing it on your own.

  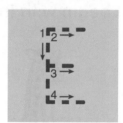 

start

Color all of the letter uppercase letter **E**'s

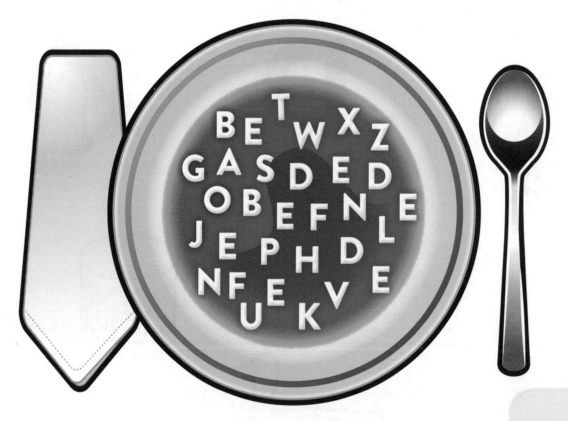

How many **E**'s
did you find?

Lowercase Letter e

Trace the lowercase letter **e**.
Then try writing it on your own.

start

Circle the words that begin
with the lowercase letter **e**.

ear	bat	bed	with
eat	won	bet	car
egg	wig	ten	see

23

Beginning Sounds

Say the name of each picture. Circle the picture that begins with the sound of the letter in each row.

Aa

Bb

Cc

Dd

Ee

Uppercase Letter F

F is for _____LY.  Trace the uppercase letter **F**.
Then try writing it on your own.

start

Find and circle all of the uppercase **F**'s in the large **F**.

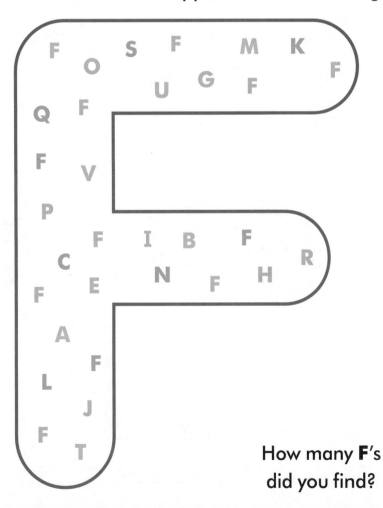

How many **F**'s
did you find?

Lowercase Letter f

Trace the lowercase letter **f**.
Then try writing it on your own.

start

Help the **f**ireman get to his **f**ire truck through the maze.

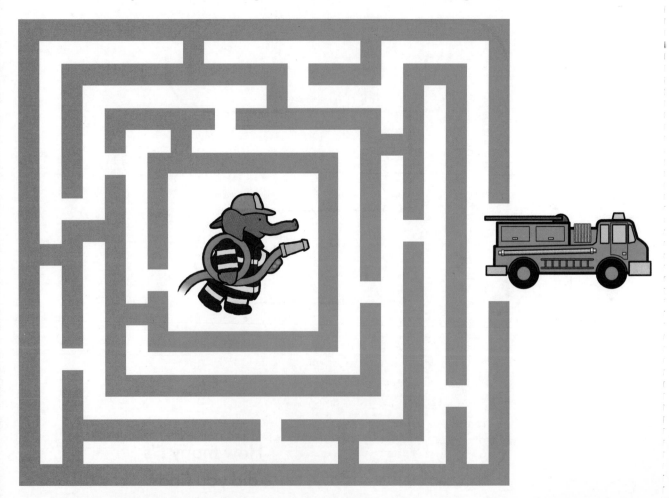

Beginning Sounds

Frog  begins with the letter **F**.
Color the **f**rog. Then draw your own picture of something
that starts with the letter **F**, such as a **f**ox or a **f**oot.

frog

Uppercase Letter G

G is for _____**IFT**.  Trace the uppercase letter **g**.
Then try writing it on your own.

start

G is for **GOAT**.
Color the letter **G**. Color the **goat**.

28

Lowercase Letter g

Trace the lowercase letter g.
Then try writing it on your own.

start

Color anything with the uppercase **G** green.
and anything with the lowercase **g** blue.

Beginning Sounds

Say the word **grapes**. **G**rapes starts with the **G** sound.
Color any pictures that begin with the **G** sound.

Uppercase Letter H

H is for _____ **EART**. Trace the uppercase letter **H**. Then try writing it on your own.

start

H is for **HEART**. Find your way through the **h**eart maze.

Lowercase Letter h

Trace the lowercase letter **h**.
Then try writing it on your own.

start

Draw a line from each uppercase **H** to a lowercase **h**.

Beginning Sounds

Say the word **honey**.  **H**oney starts with the **H** sound.
Say the name of each picture. Circle all of the pictures
that begin with the **H** sound.

H

Uppercase Letter I

I is for _____CE CREAM.  Trace the uppercase letter **I**.
Then try writing it on your own.

 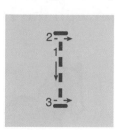  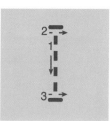

start

Ice cream begins with the letter **I**. Connect the dots
from **A** to **I** to make your own ice-cream cone.
Color it in to match your favorite flavor.

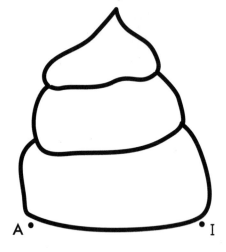

A •   • I

B • •
   C   • H
              G

D •   •   • F
         E

Lowercase Letter i

Trace the lowercase letter **i**.
Then try writing it on your own.

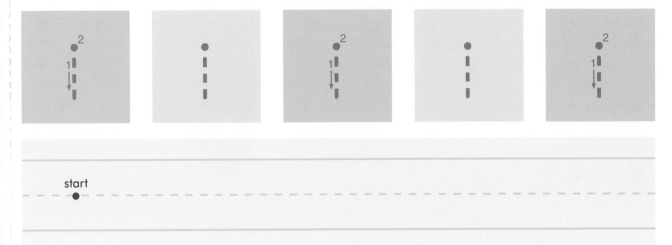

start

Color in all of the ice-cream cones
that have a lowercase **i** in them.

Beginning Sounds

Say the name of each picture. Write the uppercase letter **I** next to each picture that starts with an **I** and an uppercase letter **B** next to each picture that begins with a **B** sound. If it doesn't start with an **I** or **B**, leave it blank.

Uppercase Letter J

J is for _____ELLY.  Trace the uppercase letter **J**.
Then try writing it on your own.

start

Fill in the missing **J** to complete the words.

 _____UICE

 _____UMP ROPE

 _____ELLY BEANS

 _____ACKET

Lowercase Letter j

Trace the lowercase letter **j**.
Then try writing it on your own.

   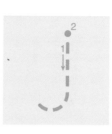 

start

Circle all of the lowercase **j**'s in the sign below.

jar	jog	lot
jaw	jet	joy
fun	jet	job

Beginning Sounds

Say the word **jaguar**. Jaguar starts with the **J** sound.
Color any pictures that begin with the **J** sound.

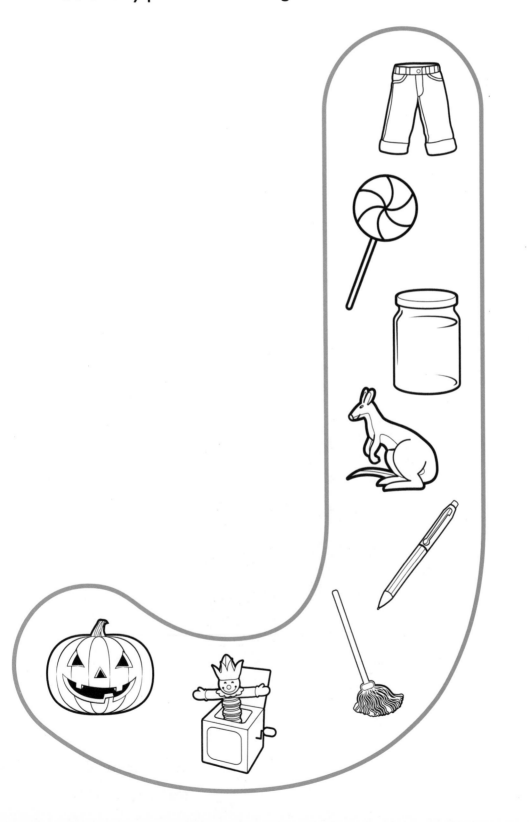

Uppercase Letter K

K is for _____**ITE.** Trace the uppercase letter **K**.
Then try writing it on your own.

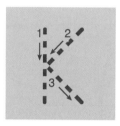  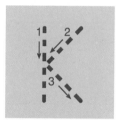  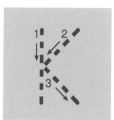

start

Color in all of the uppercase **K**s.

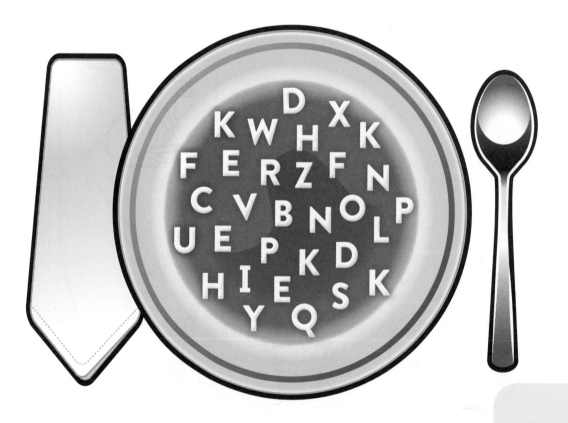

How many **K**'s
did you find?

Lowercase Letter k

Trace the lowercase letter **k**.
Then try writing it on your own.

start

Circle all of the lowercase **k**'s.
Connect the circles to complete the picture.

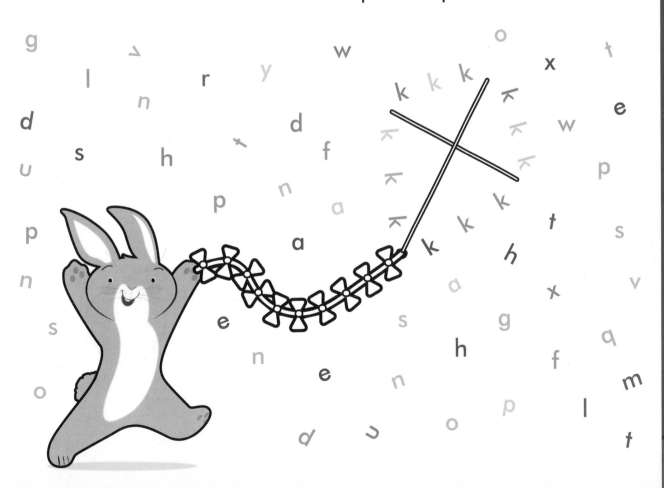

Beginning Sounds

Say the word **k**itten. **K**itten starts with the **K** sound.
Say the name of each picture. Circle all of the
pictures that begin with the **K** sound.

K

Uppercase Letter L

L is for _____ **EAF**.  Trace the uppercase letter **L**.
Then try writing it on your own.

start

L is for **LION**. Color in the **L**. Color in the **lion**.

Lowercase Letter l

Trace the lowercase letter **l**.
Then try writing it on your own.

start

It's fall! Look how beautiful the leaves are!
Color any leaf with an uppercase **L** in it **orange**
and any leaf with a lowercase **l** in it **red**.

Beginning Sounds

Say the name of each picture. Draw a line to the letter that shows the beginning sound.

C

A

B

D

L

K

H

45

Uppercase Letter M

M is for _____ ILK.  Trace the uppercase letter **M**. Then try writing it on your own.

  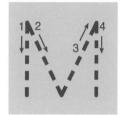 M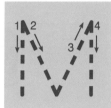

start

Color in all of the uppercase **M**'s.

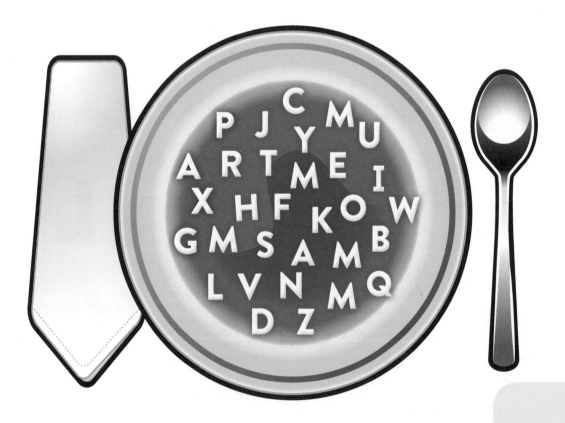

How many **M**'s did you find?

Lowercase Letter m

Trace the lowercase letter **m**.
Then try writing it on your own.

start

Draw a line from each uppercase **M** to a lowercase **m** below.

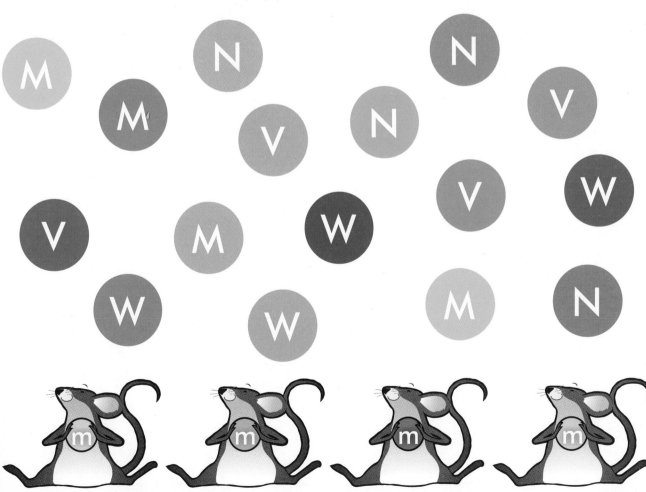

Beginning Sounds

Monkey  begins with the letter **M**.
Color the **m**onkey. Then draw your own picture of something
that starts with the letter **M**, such as the **m**oon or a **m**ouse.

monkey

Uppercase Letter N

N is for _____**EST**.  Trace the uppercase letter **N**.
Then try writing it on your own.

start

Find and circle all of the uppercase **N**'s in the large **N**.

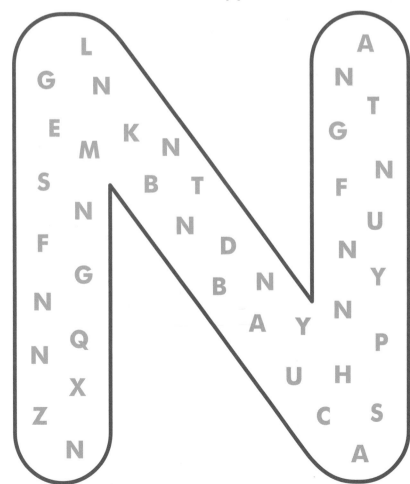

How many **N**'s
did you find?

49

Lowercase Letter n

Trace the lowercase letter **n**.
Then try writing it on your own.

start

Write the beginning letter lowercase **n** to complete the words.

 _____ ecklace

 _____ ewspapers

 _____ ose

50

Uppercase Letter P

P is for _____EAR.  Trace the uppercase letter **P**.
Then try writing it on your own.

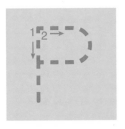   

start

P is for **PIG**. Color the letter **P**. Color the **pig**.

Lowercase Letter p

Trace the lowercase letter **p**.
Then try on writing it your own.

start

Circle all of the lowercase letter **p**'s in the sign below.
Underline any words that begin with the letter **p**.

pat	pop	top	car
zap	cow	pea	why
pan	lap	pin	one

Ending Sounds

Look at each picture and say the word out loud.
What ending sound do you hear? Write the letter
in the box below each picture.

t   g   l   m   n   f   r   x

Uppercase Letter Q

Q is for _____**UEEN**.  Trace the uppercase letter **Q**.
Then try writing it on your own.

start

Help the **QUEEN** get to her castle by following
the path of uppercase letter **Q**.

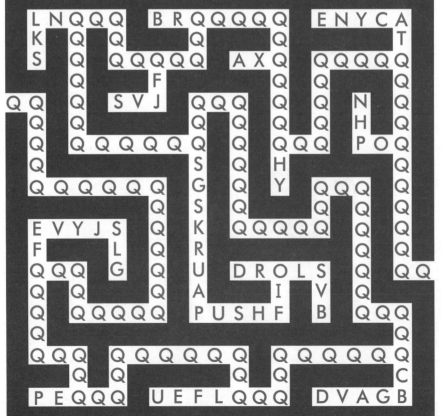

Lowercase Letter q

Trace the lowercase letter **q**.
Then try writing it on your own.

start

Help color in the beautiful quilt.
Color all the uppercase **Q**'s **red** and all the lowercase **q**'s **blue**.

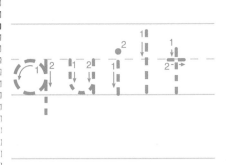

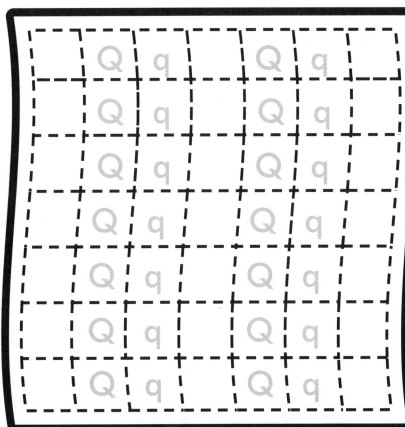

Ending Sounds

Write the missing letter for the ending sound.

n r t p d g

robo ___

skoote ___

skateboar ___

swin ___

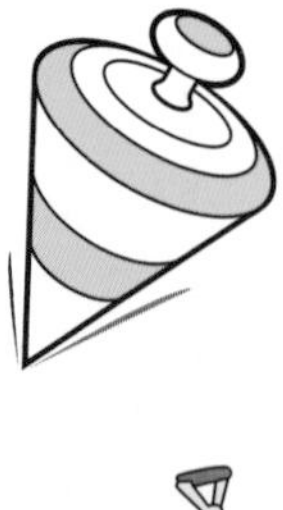

to ___

wago ___

Uppercase Letter R

R is for _____**OCKET**.  Trace the uppercase letter **R**. Then try writing it on your own.

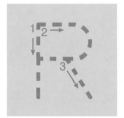  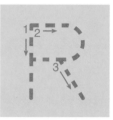

start

R is for **ROCKET**. Circle all of the uppercase letter **R**'s below.

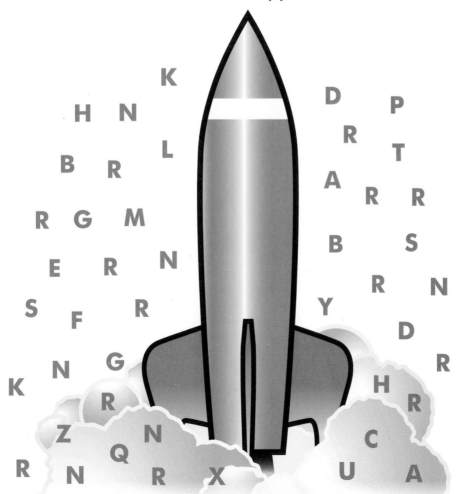

Lowercase Letter r

Trace the lowercase letter **r**.
Then try writing it on your own.

start

Color all of the raindrops with the lowercase **r blue**.

Beginning Sounds

Robot begins with the letter **R**. Color the robot. Then draw your own picture of something that starts with the letter **R**, such as a **r**ooster or a **r**abbit.

robot

Uppercase Letter S

Trace the uppercase letter **S**.
Then try writing it on your own.

start

Snake begins with the letter **S**.
Find and color all of the **s**nakes in the picture below.

How many
snakes did
you find?

Lowercase Letter s

Trace the lowercase letter **s**.
Then try writing it on your own.

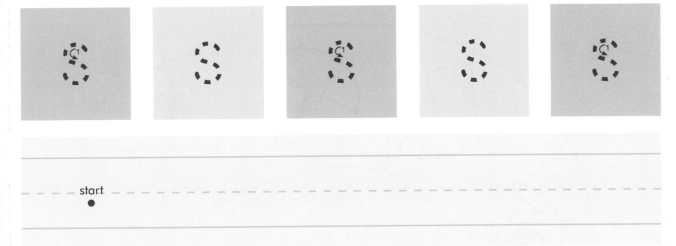

start

Color any spider with the lowercase **s black**.

Beginning Sounds

Say the word **s**un. **S**un starts with the **S** sound.
Color any pictures that begin with the **S** sound in the large **S** below.

Uppercase Letter T

T is for _____**OP**. Trace the uppercase letter **T**. Then try writing it on your own.

start

Fill in the missing **T** to complete the words.

 ____OP

 ____IGER

 ____REE

 ____OMATO

 ____RIANGLE

67

Lowercase Letter t

Trace the lowercase letter **t**.
Then try writing it on your own.

start

Color in each truck with an uppercase **T** blue
and each truck with a lowercase **t** green.

Beginning Sounds

Say the word **t**oad. 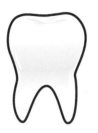 **T**oad starts with the **T** sound. Say the name of each picture. Circle all of the pictures that begin with the **T** sound.

T

Uppercase Letter U

U is for _____ **MBRELLA**.  Trace the uppercase letter **U**.
Then try writing it on your own.

   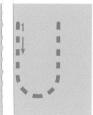

start

Find and circle all of the uppercase **U**'s inside the large **U**.

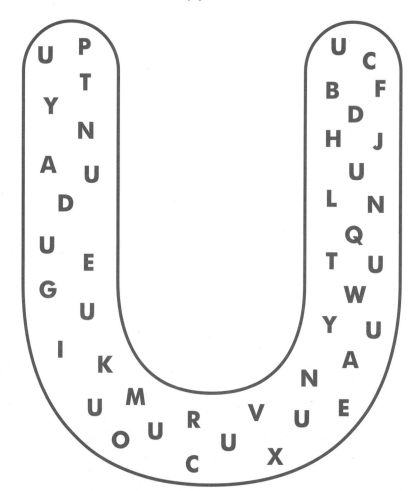

How many **U**'s did you find?

Lowercase Letter u

Trace the lowercase letter **u**.
Then try writing it on your own.

start

Color in anything with an uppercase **U** red and anything with a lowercase **u** blue to see the hidden picture!

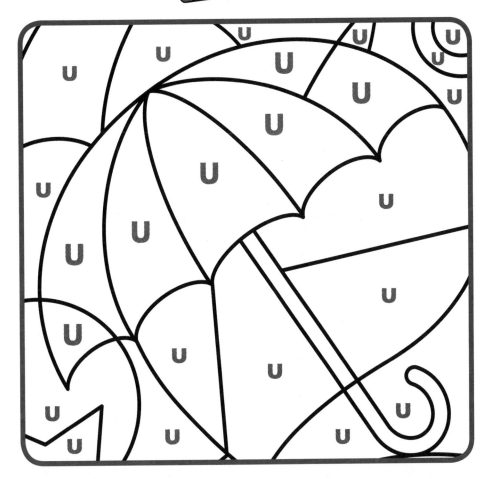

Beginning Sounds

Say the name of each picture. Circle the picture that begins with the sound of the letter in each row.

Qq

  (castle)

Rr

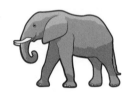 

Ss

Tt

Uu

  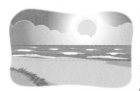

Uppercase Letter V

V is for _____IOLIN.  Trace the uppercase letter **V**.
Then try writing it on your own.

start

Color in all of the uppercase letter **V**'s.

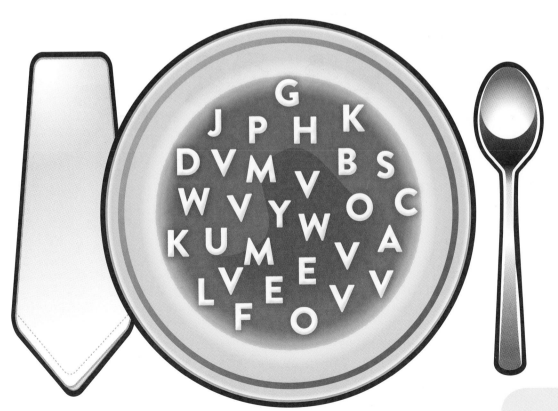

How many **V**'s
did you find?

Lowercase Letter v

Trace the lowercase letter **v**.
Then try writing it on your own.

start

Draw a line from each of the uppercase letter **V**'s to
one of the lowercase letter **v**'s in the violets below.

v W M V U V

w v v m u v

Beginning Sounds

Say the name of each picture. Draw a line to the letter that shows the beginning sound. Trace the letter.

Uppercase Letter W

W is for _____**AGON**.  Trace the uppercase letter **W**. Then try writing it on your own.

start

W is for **WOLF**. Color in the **W**. Color in the wolf.

Lowercase Letter w

Trace the lowercase letter **w**.
Then try writing it on your own.

start

Color in all of the **w**hales that have a lowercase **w** in them.

77

Beginning Sounds

Say the name of each picture. Write an uppercase letter **S** next to each picture that starts with an **S** sound and an uppercase letter **W** next to each picture that begins with the **W** sound. If it does not begin with an **S** or a **W**, leave it blank.

Uppercase Letter X

X is for _____-RAY.  Trace the uppercase letter **X**.
Then try writing it on your own.

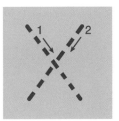  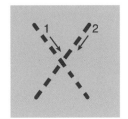 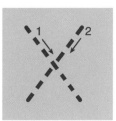

start

Find and circle all of the uppercase **X**'s in the large **X**.

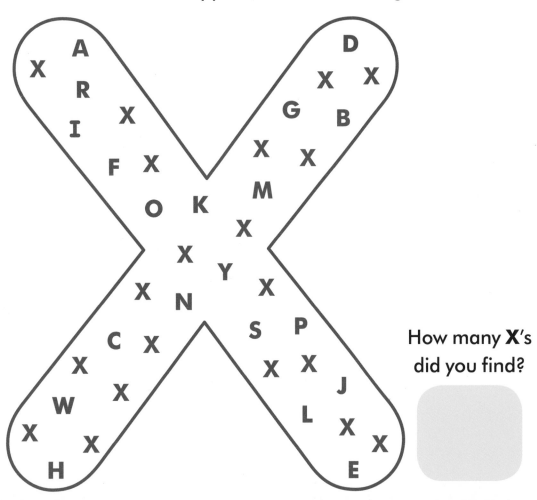

How many **X**'s
did you find?

79

Lowercase Letter x

Trace the lowercase letter **x**.
Then try writing it on your own.

start

Help the doctor give his patient an **x**-ray by showing
him the way through the maze.

Ending Sounds

Write the missing letter for the ending sound.

x l f r k r

fo ___

wol ___

dee ___

skun ___

squirre ___

bea ___

Uppercase Letter Y

Y is for _____**O-YO**. 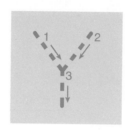 Trace the uppercase letter **Y**.
Then try writing it on your own.

   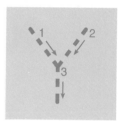

start

Color the pictures that begin with the letter **Y**.
Then add the letter **Y** to finish the word.

 _____ AK

 _____ ARN

 _____ NAKE

_____ OGURT

Uppercase Letter Z

Z is for _____**EBRA**. 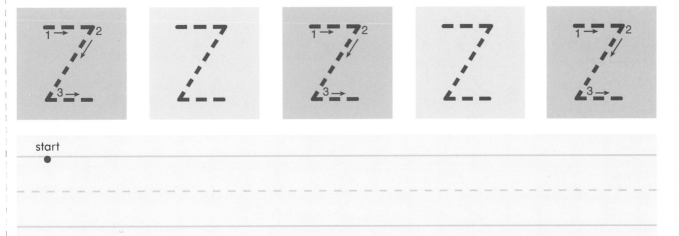 Trace the uppercase letter **Z**.
Then try writing it on your own.

start

Find and circle all of the uppercase **Z**'s hidden at the **ZOO**.

How many **Z**'s did you find?

85

Lowercase Letter z

Trace the lowercase letter **z**.
Then try writing it on your own.

start

Zippy the **Z**ebra loves to sleep!
Trace the **z**'s above his head so he can
get a good night's sleep.

SIGHT WORDS

Sight Word: AM

Trace the sight word on the dotted lines.
Write it to complete the sentence.

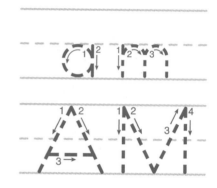

I ___ ___ excited to go to the zoo today!

am   am   am

Color the boxes with the word **am**.

am	in	are
all	am	at
is	as	am

Sight Word: WITH

Trace the sight word on the dotted lines.
Write it to complete the sentence.

I like to play tag ___ ___ ___ ___
my best friend.

with   with   with

Find the words **AM** and **WITH** two times in the word search below.
The words may go across or down.

W	P	E	F	D	I	D	A	F	L
I	J	U	A	M	D	V	M	B	K
T	T	K	H	K	I	B	F	N	O
H	O	E	M	Y	W	I	T	H	R

Sight Word: ARE

Trace the sight word on the dotted lines.
Write it to complete the sentence.

They _ _ _ waiting for the bus.

are   are   are

Color the stars with the word **are** in them.

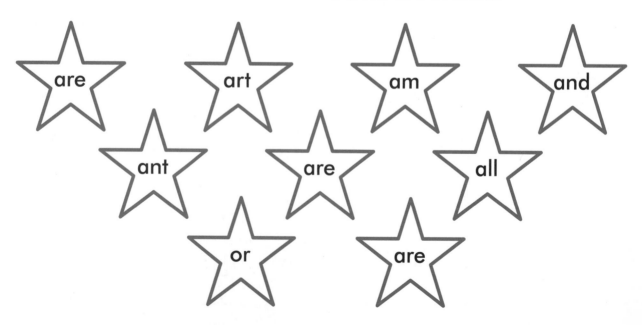

Sight Word: AT

Trace the sight word on the dotted lines.
Write it to complete the sentence.

We had fun __ __ the party!

at   at   at

Circle the sight words **are** and **at** in the sentences below.

We are at the park.

Are you going to join us?

Meet us at 12:00.

Trace the sight word on the dotted lines.
Write it to complete the sentence.

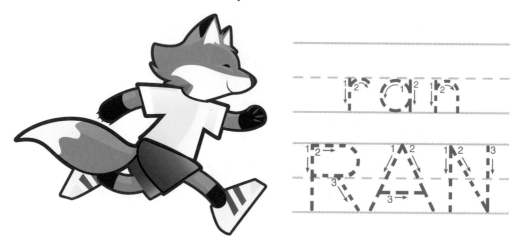

I __ __ __ all the way home.

ran ran ran

Find the words **GET** and **RAN** two times in the word search below.
The words may go across or down.

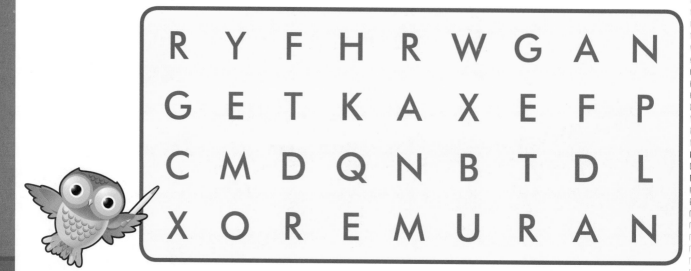

R	Y	F	H	R	W	G	A	N
G	E	T	K	A	X	E	F	P
C	M	D	Q	N	B	T	D	L
X	O	R	E	M	U	R	A	N

Sight Word: GET

Trace the sight word on the dotted lines.
Write it to complete the sentence.

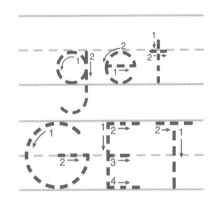

May we please ___ ___ ___
some ice cream?

 get get get

Color the boxes with the word **get**.

go	bet	get
got	get	set
met	let	but

Sight Words: DID

Trace the sight word on the dotted lines.
Write it to complete the sentence.

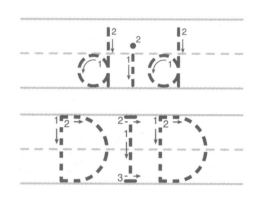

___ ___ ___ you have fun
at the playground?

did   did   did

Find the words **CAME** and **DID** two times in the word search below.
The words may go across or down.

D	I	D	U	P	E	F	D	C	C
J	D	V	W	J	U	L	I	Q	A
K	C	A	M	E	K	H	D	J	M
Y	P	S	V	O	E	M	I	N	E

Sight Word: CAME

Trace the sight word on the dotted lines.
Write it to complete the sentence.

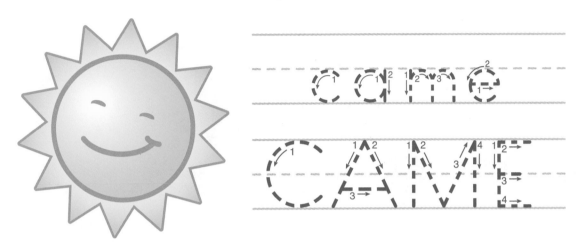

I'm glad the sun __ __ __ __ out!

came   came   came

Color the diamonds with the word **came** in them.

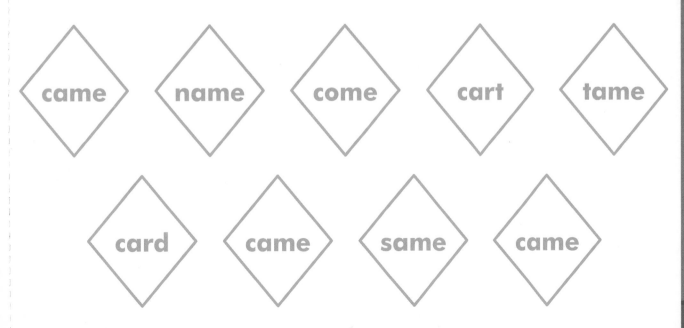

came name come cart tame

card came same came

95

Sight Word: DO

Trace the sight word on the dotted lines.
Write it to complete the sentence.

What vegetables __ __ you like to eat?

Circle the sight words **came** and **do** in the sentences below.

We came to play and have fun.

What do you like to do for fun?

Do you like to dance?

SIGHT WORDS

Sight Word: EAT

Trace the sight word on the dotted lines.
Write it to complete the sentence.

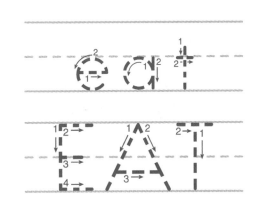

I love to ___ ___ ___ pizza!

eat   eat   eat

Color the word **eat**.

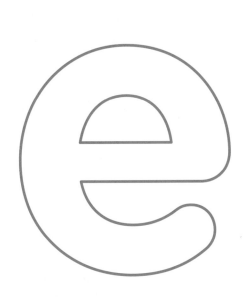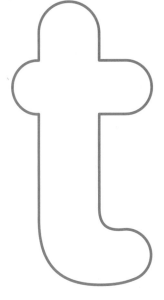

Trace the sight word on the dotted lines.
Write it to complete the sentence.

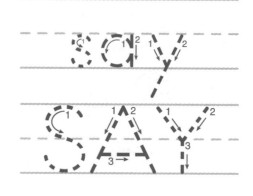

__ __ __ thank-you when someone gives you a present.

say   say   say

Color the boxes with the word **say** in them.

sat	say	are
day	may	out
say	see	hay

Sight Word: GOOD

Trace the sight word on the dotted lines.
Write it to complete the sentence.

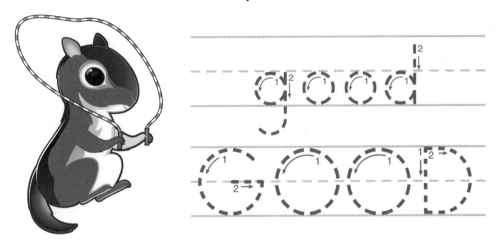

Exercise is ___ ___ ___ ___ for you!

 good    good    good

Find the words **SAY** and **GOOD** two times in the word search below.
The words may go across or down.

I	D	U	P	E	F	G	D	C	L
D	G	O	O	D	L	O	I	Q	B
I	A	J	T	K	H	O	S	A	Y
P	S	A	Y	E	M	D	I	N	Y

Sight Word: HAVE

Trace the sight word on the dotted lines.
Write it to complete the sentence.

I _ _ _ _ to take a bath.

have   have   have

Color the hearts with the word **have** in them.

have   here   save   have

there   have   had

hand   house

Sight Word: HE

Trace the sight word on the dotted lines.
Write it to complete the sentence.

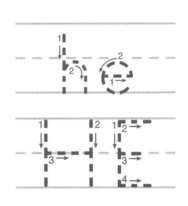

___ ___ is strong!

he	he	he

Circle the sight words **have** and **he** in the sentences below.

I have a little brother.

He is three years old.

He and I have a lot of fun together.

101

Sight Word: INTO

Trace the sight word on the dotted lines.
Write it to complete the sentence.

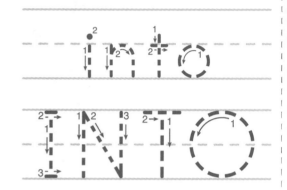

The pig fell __ __ __ __ the mud.

into   into   into

Color the word **into**.

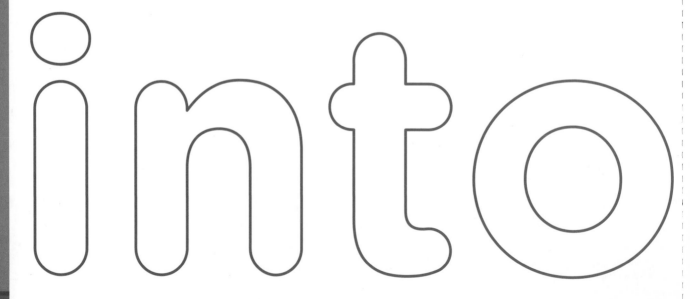

Sight Word: LIKE

Trace the sight word on the dotted lines.
Write it to complete the sentence.

Do you _ _ _ _ clowns?

like   like   like

Find the words **INTO** and **LIKE** two times in the word search below.
The words may go across or down.

B Q L I K E I K L
H G B P C K N W I
V J N M A L T R K
I N T O R E O E E

Sight Word: NEW

Trace the sight word on the dotted lines.
Write it to complete the sentence.

I got a ___ ___ ___ kite
for my birthday!

new   new   new

Find the words **WILL** and **NEW** two times in the word search below.
The words may go across or down.

W	P	E	F	N	E	W	L	D	A
I	J	N	L	O	I	Q	B	L	Z
L	T	E	H	O	G	E	T	G	X
L	T	W	M	D	I	W	I	L	L

Sight Word: WILL

Trace the sight word on the dotted lines.
Write it to complete the sentence.

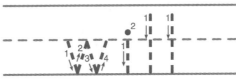

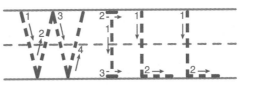

___ ___ ___ ___ you share your
cookie with me?

| will | will | will |

Color each of the circles with the word **will** in them.

will   with   why   will

were   will   who

when   what

Trace the sight word on the dotted lines.
Write it to complete the sentence.

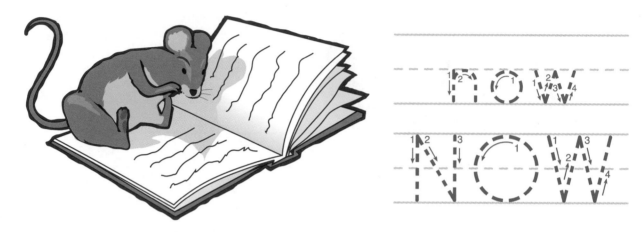

Please do your homework right __ __ __.

now   now   now

Circle the sight words **will** and **now** in the sentences below.

Will you come here right now?

We will be leaving soon.

Now it is time to go.

Sight Word: ON

Trace the sight word on the dotted lines.
Write it to complete the sentence.

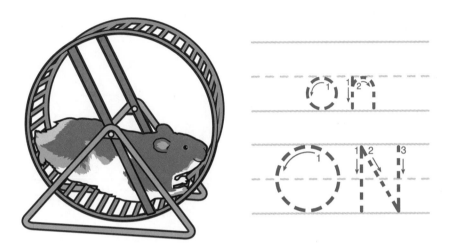

The hamster ran __ __ the wheel.

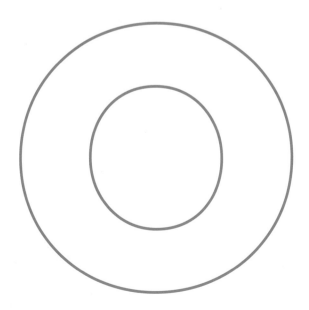

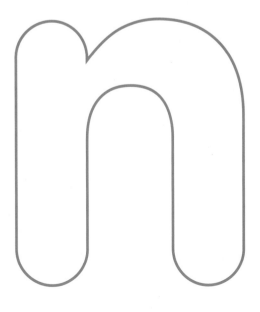

Color the word **on**.

Trace the sight word on the dotted lines.
Write it to complete the sentence.

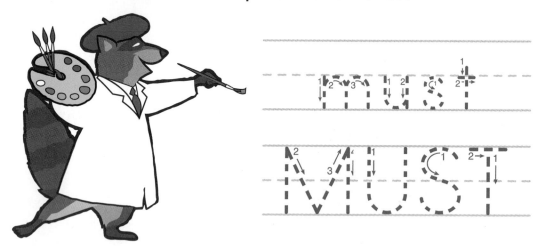

To be a good artist, you __ __ __ __ paint every day!

must   must   must

Color the boxes with the word **must** in them.

mom	must	most
must	more	much
might	dust	must

Sight Word: PLEASE

Trace the sight word on the dotted lines.
Write it to complete the sentence.

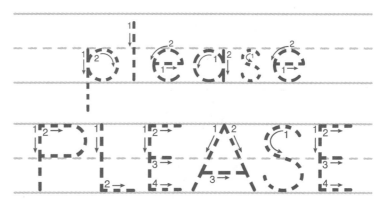

__ __ __ __ __ __ read me a book.

please   please   please

Find the words **MUST** and **PLEASE** two times in the word search below.
The words may go across or down.

G	U	W	M	T	I	M	S	T	M
L	E	F	P	L	E	A	S	E	U
M	U	S	T	I	Q	L	Z	K	S
P	L	E	A	S	E	G	X	P	T

Trace the sight word on the dotted lines.
Write it to complete the sentence.

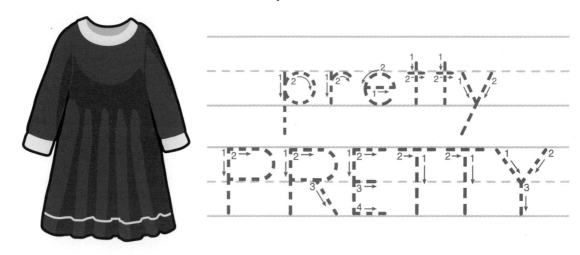

That dress is so __ __ __ __ __ __!

pretty pretty pretty

Color the squares with the word **pretty** in them.

pretty	party	please	really
	pass	silly	pretty
	pretty	pity	

Sight Word: SAW

Trace the sight word on the dotted lines.
Write it to complete the sentence.

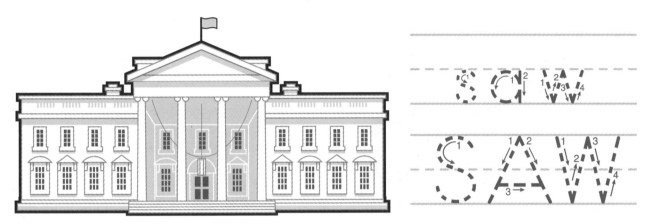

I __ __ __ the White House
in Washington, D.C.

saw   saw   saw

Circle the sight words **pretty** and **saw** in the sentences below.

I saw a pretty ladybug sitting on a leaf.

It had six pretty spots.

When it saw me, it flew away.

Trace the sight word on the dotted lines.
Write it to complete the sentence.

I like to __ __ __ __ my bike.

| ride | ride | ride |

Color the word **ride**.

Sight Word: WENT

Trace the sight word on the dotted lines.
Write it to complete the sentence.

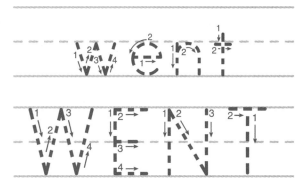

I _ _ _ _ to the
grocery store with my mom.

went   went   went

Find the words **EAT** and **WENT** two times in the word search below.
The words may go across or down.

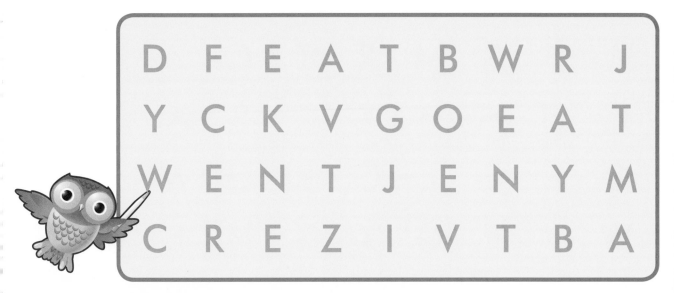

```
D  F  E  A  T  B  W  R  J
Y  C  K  V  G  O  E  A  T
W  E  N  T  J  E  N  Y  M
C  R  E  Z  I  V  T  B  A
```

Sight Word: SHE

Trace the sight word on the dotted lines.
Write it to complete the sentence.

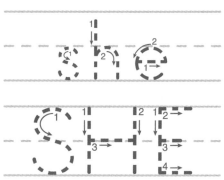

___ ___ ___ is my best friend!!

| she | she | she |

Find the words **WHO** and **SHE** two times in the word search below.
The words may go across or down.

W	F	S	M	R	T	C	Z	K	P
H	U	H	H	X	E	S	A	Y	T
O	E	E	L	G	K	U	W	H	O
W	M	E	G	X	S	H	E	R	W

114

Sight Word: WHO

Trace the sight word on the dotted lines.
Write it to complete the sentence.

__ __ __ is your teacher?

who   who   who

Color the triangles with the word **who** in them.

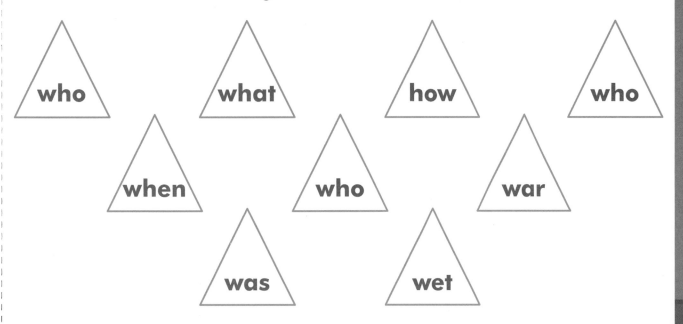

who   what   how   who

when   who   war

was   wet

SIGHT WORDS

115

Sight Word: UNDER

Trace the sight word on the dotted lines.
Write it to complete the sentence.

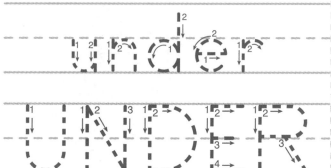

Let's look __ __ __ __ __ the
rainbow for a pot of gold!

under   under   under

Circle the sight words **too** and **under** in the sentences below.

I am standing under an umbrella.

My friend is under an umbrella, too.

We are both under an umbrella.

Trace the sight word on the dotted lines.
Write it to complete the sentence.

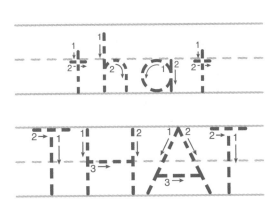

_ _ _ _ koala is in a tree.

that   that   that

Color the word **that**.

Sight Word: BUT

Trace the sight word on the dotted lines.
Write it to complete the sentence.

I like baseball, ___ ___ ___ soccer
is my favorite sport.

but	but	but

Color the boxes with the word **but**.

bun	**but**	**out**
but	**bin**	**bat**
hut	**rut**	**but**

Sight Word: THIS

Trace the sight word on the dotted lines.
Write it to complete the sentence.

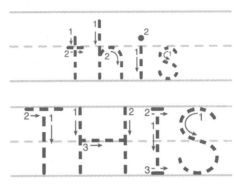

__ __ __ __ is my pet fish, Goldie.

| this | this | this |

Find the words **BUT** and **THIS** two times in the word search below.
The words may go across or down.

T	X	S	H	E	T	H	I	S	M
B	T	H	B	U	T	H	U	E	H
U	E	B	A	Y	T	Y	I	Q	L
T	K	T	H	I	S	W	M	S	G

119

Sight Word: TOO

Trace the sight word on the dotted lines.
Write it to complete the sentence.

I like to play in the rain, __ __ __!

| too | too | too |

Color the stars with the word **too** in them.

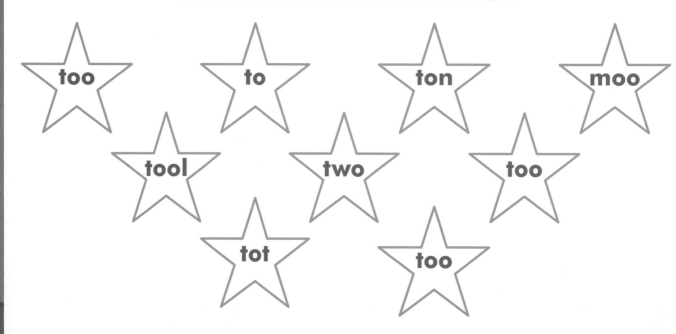

too   to   ton   moo

tool   two   too

tot   too

Trace the sight word on the dotted lines.
Write it to complete the sentence.

__ __ __ __ it will be winter!

soon   soon   soon

Circle the sight words **who** and **soon** in the sentences below.

Soon I will leave for camp.

I wonder who comes next.

Who will be in my cabin?

SIGHT WORDS

Trace the sight word on the dotted lines.
Write it to complete the sentence.

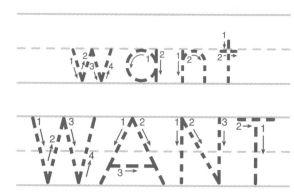

I _ _ _ _ to find a secret treasure!

want   want   want

Color the word **want**.

want

Sight Word: OUR

Trace the sight word on the dotted lines.
Write it to complete the sentence.

This is _____ mail carrier.

our   our   our

Find the words **WANT** and **OUR** two times in the word search below.
The words may go across or down.

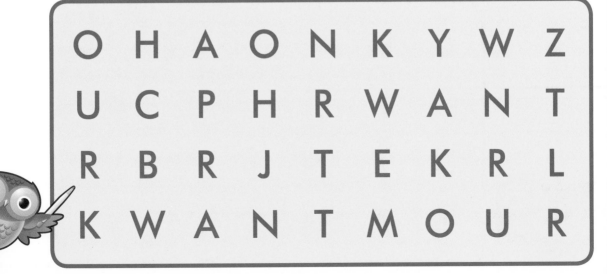

O H A O N K Y W Z
U C P H R W A N T
R B R J T E K R L
K W A N T M O U R

123

Sight Word: NO

Trace the sight word on the dotted lines.
Write it to complete the sentence.

___ ___, I do not like snakes.

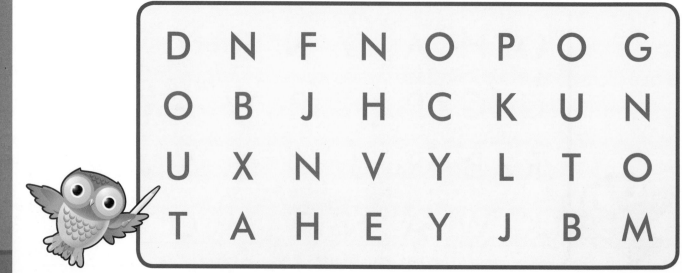

no   no   no

Find the words **OUT** and **NO** two times in the word search below.
The words may go across or down.

D	N	F	N	O	P	O	G
O	B	J	H	C	K	U	N
U	X	N	V	Y	L	T	O
T	A	H	E	Y	J	B	M

Sight Word: OUT

Trace the sight word on the dotted lines.
Write it to complete the sentence.

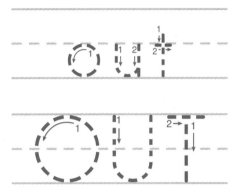

Let's play when we get ___ ___ ___
of school.

Color the boxes with the word **out**.

out	our	off
ate	too	out
owl	out	own

125

Trace the sight word on the dotted lines.
Write it to complete the sentence.

_____ ___ ___, it is my birthday.

yes   yes   yes

Color the word **yes**.

Sight Word: THERE

Trace the sight word on the dotted lines.
Write it to complete the sentence.

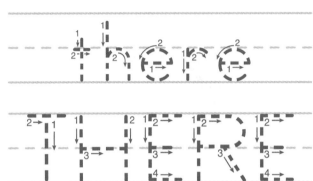

I stop ___ ___ ___ ___ ___ on the way home.

there   there   there

Find the words **YES** and **THERE** two times in the word search below.
The words may go across or down.

```
Y  Q  L  Y  T  H  E  R  E
E  G  B  I  C  K  W  N  W
S  J  N  M  K  L  Q  B  N
T  H  E  R  E  Y  E  S  T
```

127

Sight Word: WAS

Trace the sight word on the dotted lines.
Write it to complete the sentence.

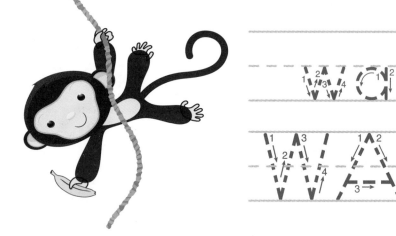

The monkey __ __ __ swinging from the tree.

was   was   was

Find the words **THEY** and **WAS** two times in the word search below.
The words may go across or down.

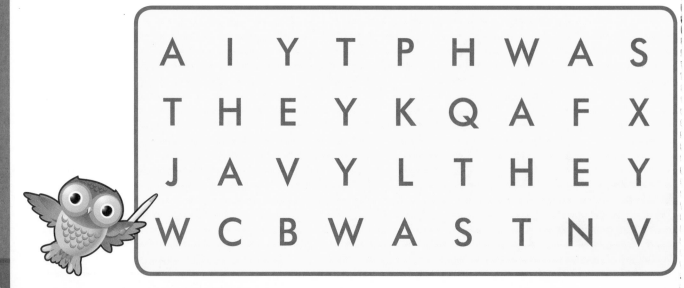

A I Y T P H W A S
T H E Y K Q A F X
J A V Y L T H E Y
W C B W A S T N V

128

Sight Word: THEY

Trace the sight word on the dotted lines.
Write it to complete the sentence.

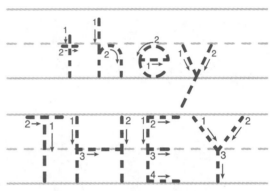

Are _ _ _ _ going to the beach?

they	they	they

Color the boxes with the word **they**.

they	that	them
tray	they	then
this	the	they

SIZES, COMPARISONS, & OPPOSITES

Same Size

Look at the pictures of vegetables in each row.
Circle the picture of the vegetable in each row that
is the **same size** as the picture at left.

Draw a triangle in the box the exact
same size as the orange triangle.

Different Size

Look at the picture of the bugs in each row.
Circle the picture of the bug in each row that
is a **different size** than the first picture.

Bigger and Smaller

Look at the musical instruments in each box.
Color in the one that is **bigger**.

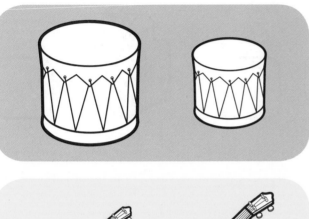

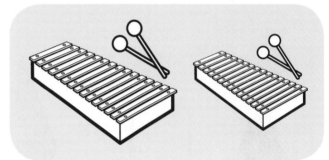

Look at the musical instruments in each box.
Color in the one that is **smaller**.

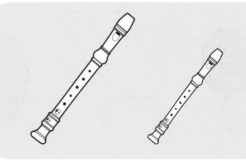

Bigger and Smaller

Number the items 1, 2, or 3 from **smallest** to **biggest**.

Slower or Faster

A turtle is **slow**.
A turtle is **slower** than a rabbit.

A rabbit is **fast**.
A rabbit is **faster** than a turtle.

Circle the correct answer.

panther   cat

A panther is **slower faster** than a cat.

deer   cow

A deer is **slower faster** than a cow.

crab   shark

A crab is **slower faster** than a shark.

frog   worm

A frog is **slower faster** than a worm.

Trace the words **left** and **right** below. Now look at your hands and say which one is **left** and which one is **right**.

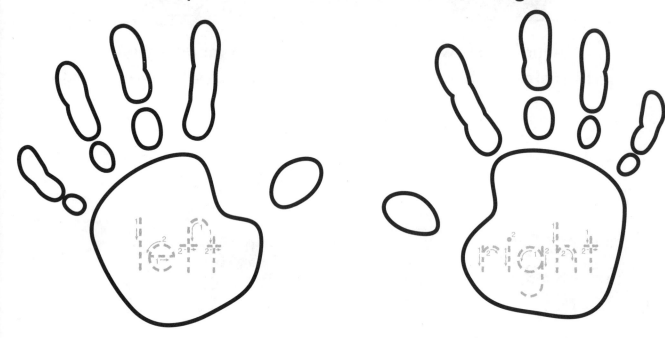

Color the birds on the **left** side of the tree **red**.
Color the birds on the **right** side of the tree **blue**.

What Goes Together?

Look at the pictures in each row. Three of the items go together and one does not. Draw an **X** over the item that does not go with the rest.

  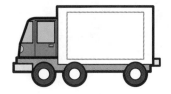 

What Goes Together?

Draw a line from the things in the top row that go together with those in the bottom row.

Draw something in the box below that goes with a barn.

Find the Pattern

Look at the patterns below. Circle **yes** if the patterns are the same. Circle **no** if the patterns are different.

Are these patterns the same?   Yes   No

Are these patterns the same?   Yes   No

Are these patterns the same?   Yes   No

139

Find the Match

All the snowmen are different except for two.
Find the match. Circle the two snowmen
that are exactly **the same**.

Match the Pictures That Rhyme

Draw a line from the picture on the left to the picture of the thing that **rhymes** with it on the right.

lock

phone

cat

star

bone

mouse

car

clock

house

hat

Words That Rhyme

Draw a line from each word on the left to the
word that **rhymes** with it on the right.

corn

can

school

wig

pig

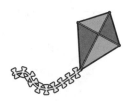

kite

light

pool

van

horn

Same Size

Circle the picture of the animal in each row that is the **same size** as the picture at the left.

Draw a circle in the box below the exact **same size** as the purple circle.

Different Size

Circle the picture of the animal in each row that is a **different size** than the picture at left.

Top, Middle, & Bottom

Color the top light **red** which means stop.
Color the middle light **yellow**, which means caution.
Color the bottom light **green**, which means go.

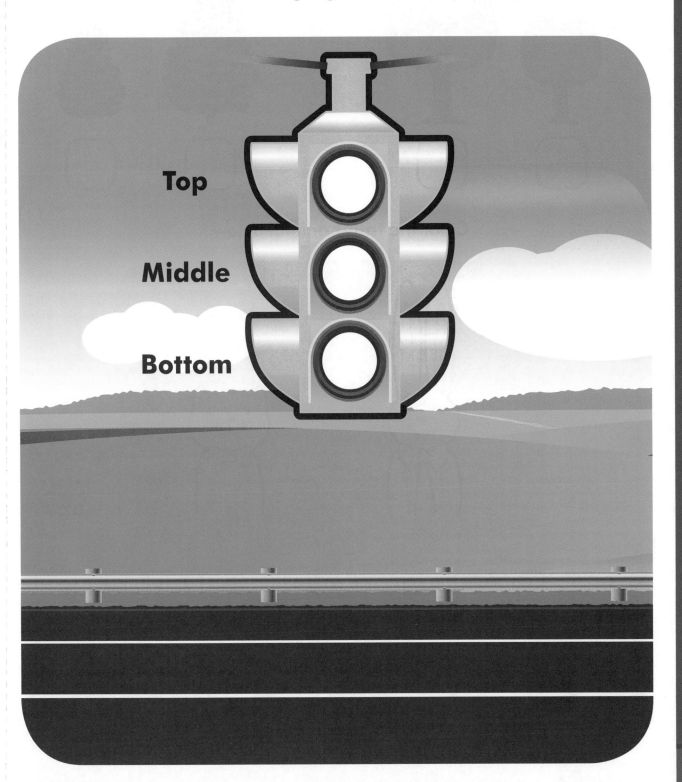

Top

Middle

Bottom

Shorter & Taller

Put an **X** under the **shorter** tree.

Color the **taller** animal below.

Complete the sentence with either **short** or **tall**.

 He is   **short**   **tall**.

 She is   **short**   **tall**.

In & Out

Trace the words **in** and **out**.

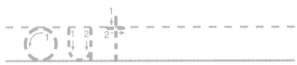

Write **in** or **out** in the following sentences.

The  is _____ the mailbox.

The 🕷 is _____ of the web.

The 🐿 is _____ the tree.

The 🦆 is _____ of the water.

147

Up & Down

Circle **up** or **down** in the following sentences.

The bear is   **up**   **down**   on the seesaw.

The fox is   **up**   **down**   on the seesaw.

The turtle swims

up   **down**.

The turtle swims

up   **down**.

Opposites

Look carefully at the pictures and draw a line connecting each word to its **opposite**.

 asleep

cold

 slow

strong

 happy

awake

 weak

fast

open

sad

hot

closed

Opposites

Look carefully at the pictures and draw a line
connecting each word to its **opposite**.

 clean

 night

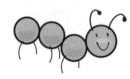 short

 back

 day

 full

 front

 dirty

 empty

long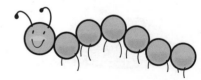

Patterns

Look at the pictures below. There is a **pattern** in each row.
Once you have figured out the **pattern**, circle what comes next.

          or

     or

           or

        or

Shape Patterns

Help the crab get to the ocean by following the
shape pattern triangle ▲, circle ●, square ■ in the maze below.

Find the Pattern

Look at the **patterns** in each column, running top to bottom.
Circle **yes** if the **patterns** are the same.
Circle **no** if the **patterns** are different.

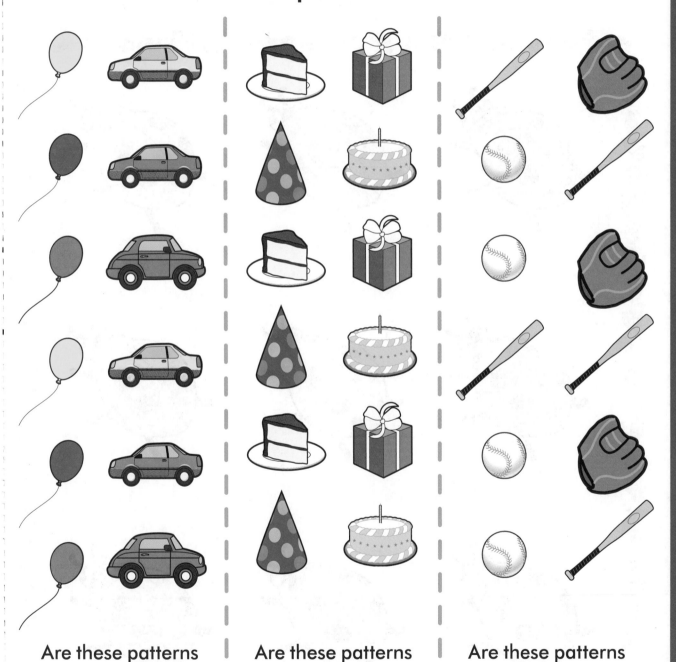

Are these patterns
the same?

Yes   No

Are these patterns
the same?

Yes   No

Are these patterns
the same?

Yes   No

All of the ladybugs below are different except for two.
Find the match. Circle the two ladybugs
that are exactly **the same**.

Match the Pictures That Rhyme

Draw a line from the picture on the left to the picture of the thing that **rhymes** with it on the right.

block

car

nail

kittens

star

mail

snake

sock

mittens

rake

Words That Rhyme

Draw a line from each word on the left to the word that **rhymes** with it on the right.

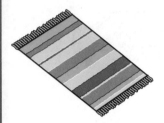 rug fruit

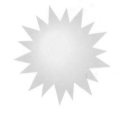 sun fun

 dish bug

 ball tall

 suit fish

156

Same Size

Look at the pictures in each box.
Circle the pictures that are the **same size**.

Different Size

Look at the picture of the bugs in each row.
Circle the picture of the one bug in each row that
is a **different size** than the picture at left.

Bigger and Smaller

Look at the objects in each box and color in the one that is **bigger**.

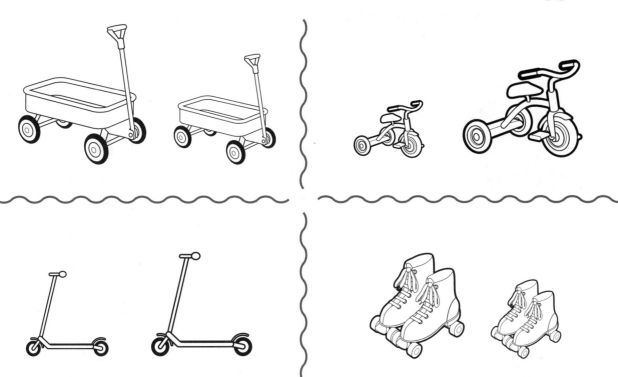

Look at the objects in each box and color in the one that is **smaller**.

159

Bigger and Smaller

In each row, draw an **X** through the **biggest** animal and **circle** the **smallest** animal.

Wet or Dry?

Look at the picture and then circle whether the animal lives in a **wet** or a **dry** environment.

wet   dry

wet   dry

wet   dry

wet   dry

wet   dry

wet   dry

Hot or Cold?

Draw a line from each picture to the thermometer that is either **hot** or **cold**.

COLD

HOT

Over and Under

Trace the words **over** and **under** and then write them on your own.

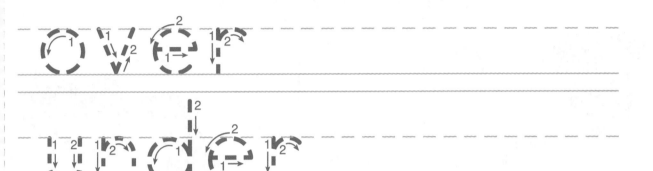

The bee is **over** the flower.

The worm is **under** the flower.

Color the spider **over** the web **black**.
Color the spider **under** the web **brown**.

Full or Empty?

Look at each picture. Draw a line from the **full** box to each of the items that are **full**. Then draw a line from the **empty** box to each of the items that are **empty**.

Patterns

Look at the pictures below.
There is a pattern in each row, running from top to bottom.
Once you have figured out the pattern, circle what comes next.

or   **or**   **or**   **or**

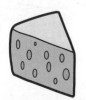   

Shape Patterns

Help the frog get to the lily pad by following this **shape pattern** ● ■ ♥ in the maze below.

Things That Go Together

Look at the pictures in each row. Three of the items go together and one does not. Draw an **X** over the item that does **not** go with the rest.

167

Things That Go Together

Draw a line from the object in the top row
to the object in the bottom row it goes with.

Draw something in the box that goes with a scarf.

Numbers

Count each group of shapes and add them together.
Write your answer on the line.

♥♥ + ♥♥♥ = ♥♥♥♥♥

2 + 3 = _____

★★★★ + ★ = ★★★★★

4 + 1 = _____

◆ + ◆◆◆ = ◆◆◆◆

1 + 3 = _____

▲▲ + ▲ = ▲▲▲▲

2 + 2 = _____

Greater Than or Less Than

Alligators are hungry animals. They always want to eat the bigger number. Think of the open end of the symbol < as the open mouth of an alligator trying to eat the bigger number.

 3   4

Now you try. Have the alligator eat the bigger number. Draw a < if the number on the right is bigger or a > if the number on the left is bigger. The first one is done for you.

3  1   1  4   5  2   3  4

3 Three

Trace the number **3** and the word **three**.

How many ones do you count?

Count the balloons and color the balloon labeled number **3**.

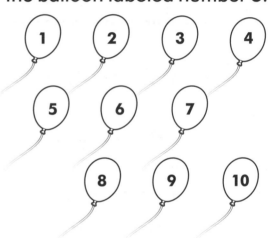

1 2 3 4
5 6 7
8 9 10

Circle all the number **3**'s.

3
4
3
6
3
7
1
5
3
7
9
5
2
3
8
4
3
3
1
8
3
6
3
2

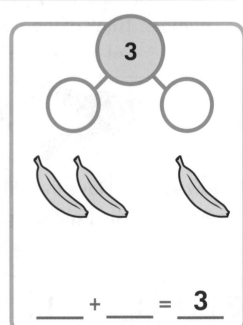

3

_____ + _____ = _3_

1 2 3 4 5 6 7 8 9

4 Four

Trace the number **4** and the word **four**.

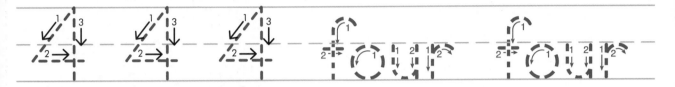

How many ones do you count?

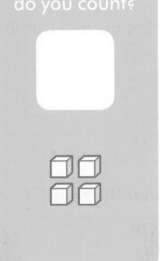

Count the bats and color the bat labeled number **4**.

Circle all the number **4**'s.

2		6	4		9
	5			2	
		3			
	7		5	4	6
1		4			3
	8		7		
				1	
4		8			4
	9		4		

4

_____ + _____ = __4__

Numbers

Tally marks are used to count or keep score. They are grouped in sets of five, which makes counting faster. Each | mark equals 1. After there are four | marks, a / mark crosses through them, which equals five.

1	I	6	⳾⳾⳾⳾ I
2	II	7	⳾⳾⳾⳾ II
3	III	8	⳾⳾⳾⳾ III
4	IIII	9	⳾⳾⳾⳾ IIII
5	⳾⳾⳾⳾	10	⳾⳾⳾⳾ ⳾⳾⳾⳾

Count the tally marks and circle the correct number.

III

1   2   3   4

IIII

1   2   3   4

- -

Circle the third frog. Draw a line under the fourth frog.

- -

Circle the number of fish in each bowl.

1   2   3   4

1   2   3   4

1   2   3   4

1   2   3   4

1   2   3   4

SKIP-COUNT BY
2's.

SAY THE NUMBERS OUT LOUD.

2

4

6

8

COLOR IN NUMBERS 3 AND 4

1   2   3   4   5   6   7   8   9

NUMBERS & COUNTING

Numbers

Look at the numbers in each row below and finish the pattern.

1   2   3   1   2 _____

3   4   3   4   3 _____

1   2   1   2   1 _____

Count each item and add them together. Write your answer on the line.

1 + 3 = _____

2 + 2 = _____

4 + 1 = _____

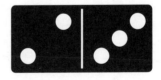

2 + 3 = _____

10   11   12   13   14   15   16   17   18   19   20

5 Five

Trace the number 5 and the word five.

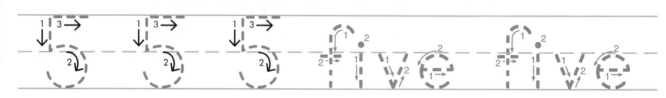

How many ones do you count?

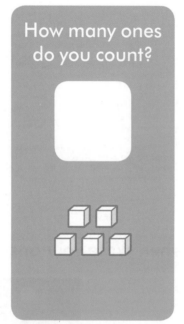

Count the pails and color the pail labeled number 5.

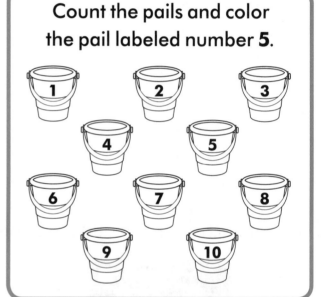

Circle all the number 5's.

5 6 2 5
 3
1   9
  4
 5   5 9 4
8   8
 7 6 2
     5
5 3
 1 7   5

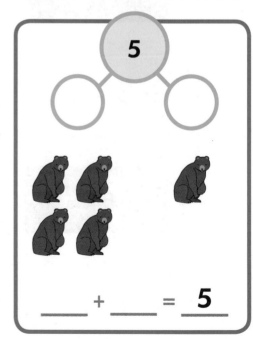

5

_____ + _____ = __5__

6 Six

Trace the number **6** and the word **six**.

How many ones do you count?

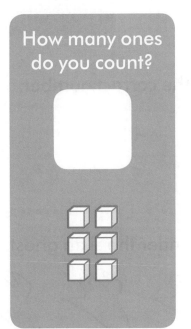

Count the hives and color the hive labeled number **6**.

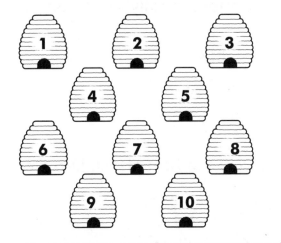

Circle all the number **6**'s.

6   8   4
  1   2   6
3   6
  5   5   1   4
1   7
  6   6   2
8   9   7
  3   9   6

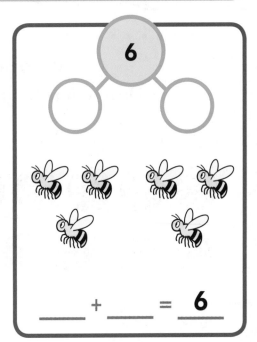

6

____ + ____ = ____ **6**

10 11 12 13 14 15 16 17 18 19 20

Numbers

Tally marks are used to count or keep score. They are grouped in sets of five, which makes counting faster. Each | mark equals 1. After there are four | marks, a / mark crosses through them, which equals five.

1	I	6	̶H̶H̶ I
2	II	7	̶H̶H̶ II
3	III	8	̶H̶H̶ III
4	IIII	9	̶H̶H̶ IIII
5	̶H̶H̶	10	̶H̶H̶ ̶H̶H̶

Count the tally marks and circle the correct number.

̶H̶H̶   ̶H̶H̶ I

3   4   5   6   3   4   5   6

Circle the fifth ghost. Draw a line under the sixth ghost.

Count the balls in each row.
Draw a line to the matching number.

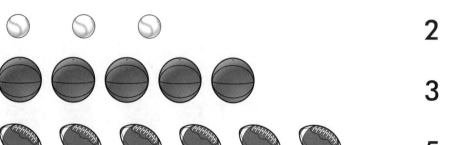

2

3

5

6

SKIP-COUNT BY

2's.

SAY THE NUMBERS OUT LOUD.

2
4
6
8
10
12
14
16

COLOR IN NUMBERS 5 AND 6

 ☆1 ☆2 ☆3 ☆4 ☆5 ☆6 ☆7 ☆8 ☆9

Numbers

Find the numbers in the word search below.
The words may run across or down.

ONE

TWO

THREE

FOUR

FIVE

Z	E	L	T	H	R	E	E	K	X
F	O	U	R	O	T	L	I	M	V
J	K	T	A	X	M	L	H	N	E
E	O	O	N	I	N	P	J	T	R
N	P	N	D	O	N	B	P	W	T
B	F	E	A	F	I	V	E	O	Y

Count each item and add them together. Write your answer on the line.

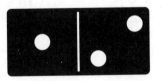

1 + 2 = _____

3 + 2 = _____

0 + 4 = _____

1 + 3 = _____

10 11 12 13 14 15 16 17 18 19 20

7 Seven

Trace the number **7** and the word **seven**.

7 7 7 seven seven

How many ones do you count?

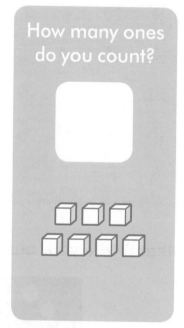

Count the birds and color the the bird labeled number **7**.

Circle all the number **7**'s.

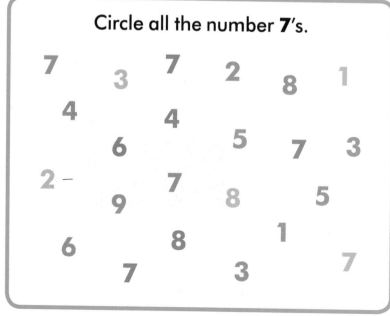

7	3	7	2	8	1
4		4			
	6		5	7	3
2		7			5
	9		8		
		8		1	
6			3		7
	7				

7

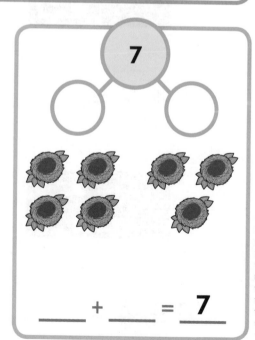

____ + ____ = **7**

COLOR IN
NUMBERS
7 AND 8

1 2 3 4 5 6 7 8 9

NUMBERS & COUNTING

184

8 Eight

Trace the number **8** and the word **eight**.

How many ones do you count?

Count the cakes and color the cake labeled number 8.

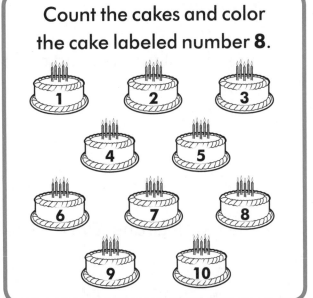

1 2 3
4 5
6 7 8
9 10

Circle all the number 8's.

7   4   8   6
  1   2
4   6
  8   3   7   8
3   9
  5   8   9
    5   2
8
  9   1   8

8

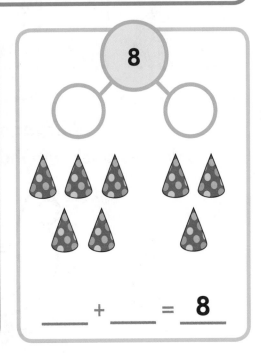

____ + ____ = __8__

☆10 ☆11 ☆12 ☆13 ☆14 ☆15 ☆16 ☆17 ☆18 ☆19 ☆20

Numbers

Tally marks are used to count or keep score. They are grouped in sets of five, which makes counting faster. Each | mark equals 1. After there are four | marks, a / mark crosses through them, which equals five.

1	I	6	HHT I
2	II	7	HHT II
3	III	8	HHT III
4	IIII	9	HHT IIII
5	HHT	10	HHT HHT

Count the tally marks and circle the correct number.

HHT II

5   6   7   8

HHT IIII

5   6   7   8

Circle the fourth giraffe. Draw a line under the eighth giraffe.

Larger or Smaller
Color the chick with the smaller number yellow.

SKIP-COUNT BY
2's.

SAY THE NUMBERS
OUT LOUD.

2
4
6
8
10
12
14
16
18
20

COLOR IN
NUMBERS
7 AND 8

★ 1 ★ 2 ★ 3 ★ 4 ★ 5 ★ 6 ★ 7 ★ 8 ★ 9

Numbers

The **+** sign means you should add. Look at each of the groups below and count the number of animals in each one. Write the correct number on the lines provided and then add the two numbers together to get the sum, or the total.

_____ + _____ = _____

_____ + _____ = _____

_____ + _____ = _____

Greater Than or Less Than

Alligators are hungry animals. They always want to eat the bigger number. Think of the open end of the symbol < as the open mouth of an alligator trying to eat the bigger number.

Now you try. Have the alligator eat the bigger number. Draw a < if the number on the right is bigger or a > if the number on the left is bigger. The first one has been done for you.

4 > 1   2 ◯ 3   5 ◯ 4   2 ◯ 4

★10 ★11 ★12 ★13 ★14 ★15 ★16 ★17 ★18 ★19 ★20

9 Nine

Trace the number **9** and the word **nine**.

How many ones do you count?

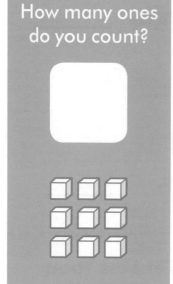

Count the butterflies and color the butterfly labeled number **9**.

Circle all the number **9**s.

2		9	8		3
	5			2	
3		5			
	9		9	7	9
7		6			
	4		4		8
				2	
1		9			9
	6		1		

9

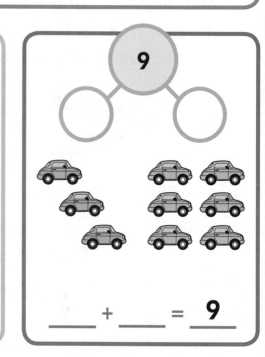

_____ + _____ = **9**

1 2 3 4 5 6 7 8 9

10 Ten

Trace the number **10** and the word **ten**.

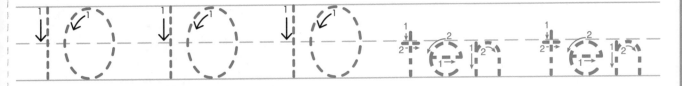

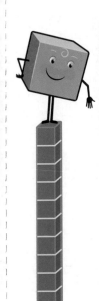

How many **ones** do you count?

How many **tens** do you count?

Count the pumpkins and color the pumpkin labeled number **10**.

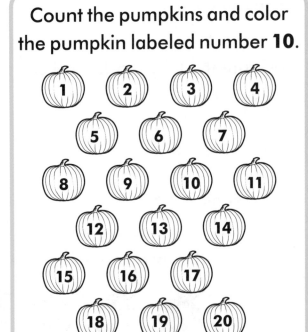

Circle all the number **10**'s.

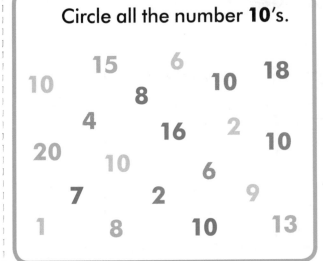

15   6
10   10   18
        8
    4
        16   2
20   10
    10   6
    7   2   9
1   8   10   13

10

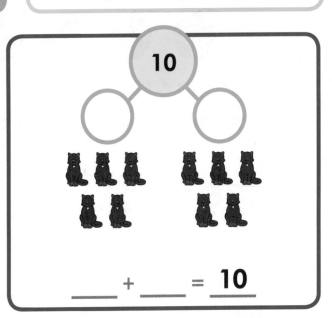

_____ + _____ = **10**

10 11 12 13 14 15 16 17 18 19 20

Numbers

Tally marks are used to count or keep score. They are grouped in sets of five, which makes counting faster. Each | mark equals 1. After there are four | marks, a / mark crosses through them, which equals five.

1	I	6	⊬ll I
2	II	7	⊬ll II
3	III	8	⊬ll III
4	IIII	9	⊬ll IIII
5	⊬ll	10	⊬ll ⊬ll

Count the tally marks and circle the correct number.

⊬ll IIII   ⊬ll ⊬ll

8   9   10   11   8   9   10   11

SKIP-COUNT BY
2's.

SAY THE NUMBERS
OUT LOUD.

Circle the ninth apple.
Draw a line under the tenth apple.

Write these numbers in order. Start with the smallest number.

5   9   3   4

2   10   6   7

COLOR IN
NUMBERS
9 AND 10

Numbers

Count the bugs below. Write the number of bugs in each row in the box at right.

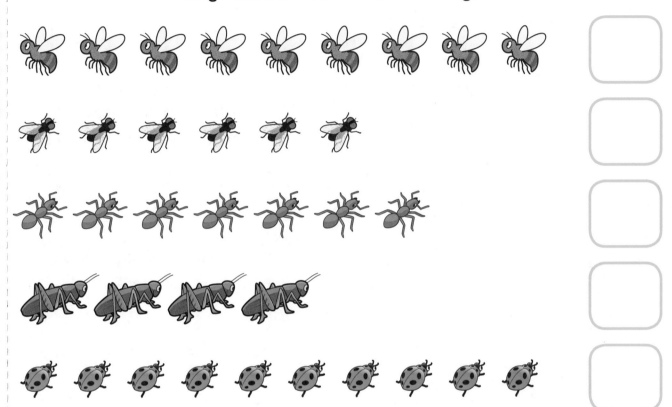

Fill in the missing numbers below.

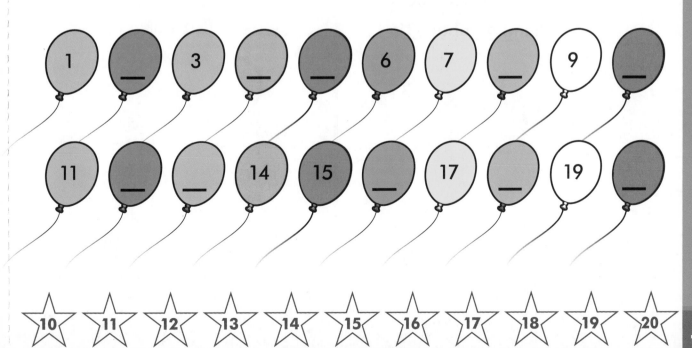

⭐10 ⭐11 ⭐12 ⭐13 ⭐14 ⭐15 ⭐16 ⭐17 ⭐18 ⭐19 ⭐20

11 Eleven

Trace the number **11** and the word **eleven**.

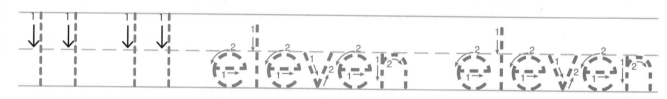

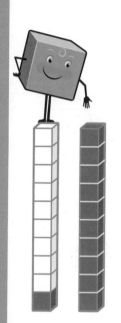

How many **ones** do you count?

How many **tens** do you count?

Countt hec hicksa ndco lor thec hickl abeledn umber**11** .

1	2	3	4
5	6	7	8
9	10	11	12
13	14	15	16
17	18	19	20

Circle all the number **11**'s.

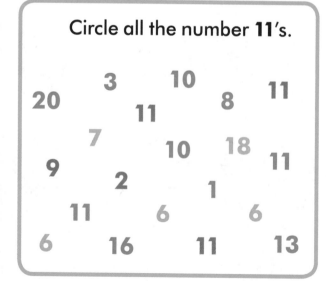

20 3 10 8 11
11
7 10 18 11
9
2 1
11 6 6
6 16 11 13

11

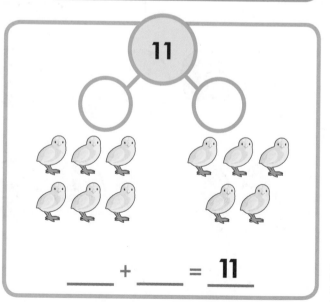

____ + ____ = **11**

 1
 2
 3
 4
 5
 6
 7
 8
 9

12 Twelve

Trace the number **12** and the word **twelve**.

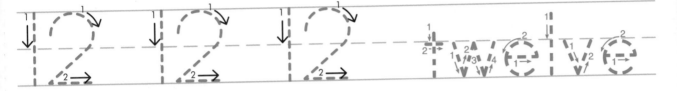

How many **ones** do you count?

How many **tens** do you count?

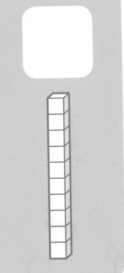

Count the chickens and color the chicken labeled number **12**.

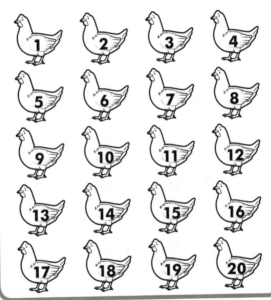

Circle all the number **12**'s.

12 1 6 4
     12
13
8 12 9 7
10
3 20
17 16 2
5 12 11 12

12

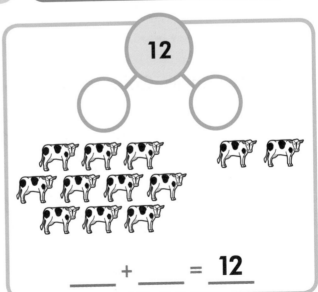

_____ + _____ = **12**

Numbers

Tally marks are used to count or keep score. They are grouped in sets of five, which makes counting faster. Each | mark equals 1. After there are four | marks, a / mark crosses through them, which equals five.

1	|	6	⦀⦀ |
2	||	7	⦀⦀ ||
3	|||	8	⦀⦀ |||
4	||||	9	⦀⦀ ||||
5	⦀⦀	10	⦀⦀ ⦀⦀

Count the tally marks and circle the correct number.

⦀⦀ ⦀⦀ |

9   10   11   12

⦀⦀ ⦀⦀ \|\|

9   10   11   12

SKIP-COUNT BY
2's.

SAY THE NUMBERS
OUT LOUD.

Circle the eighth guitar. Draw a line under the twelfth guitar.

Count the pencils. Color a square for each pencil on the graph below.

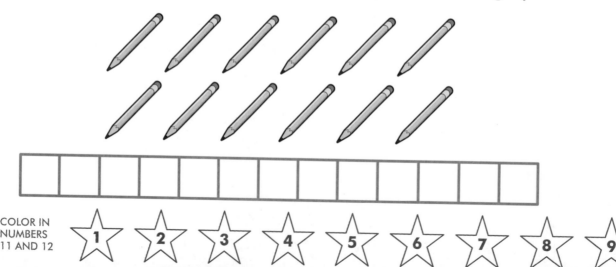

COLOR IN
NUMBERS
11 AND 12

☆1 ☆2 ☆3 ☆4 ☆5 ☆6 ☆7 ☆8 ☆9

Numbers

Count the shells on the beach. Fill in the boxes of the graph to show the number of shells.

Circle which shell appears on the beach more:

	1	2	3	4	5	6	7	8	9	10	11

Write these numbers in order from smallest to largest.

3   6   4   9

9   2   5   1

8   7   10   2

13 Thirteen

Trace the number **13** and the word **thirteen**.

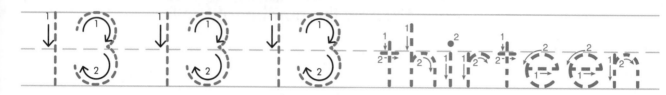

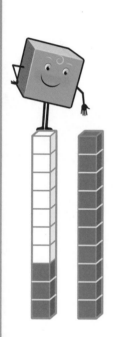

How many **ones** do you count?

How many **tens** do you count?

Count the rabbits and color the rabbit labeled number 13.

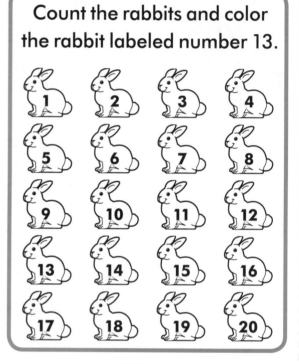

Circle all the number **13**'s.

13
7
10
2
4
12
1
13
15
18
8
17
6
5
9
13
14
13
16
20

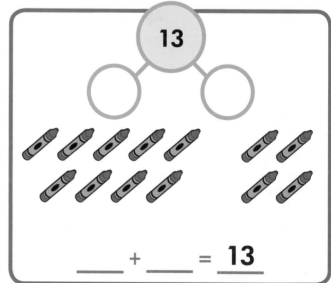

13

____ + ____ = **13**

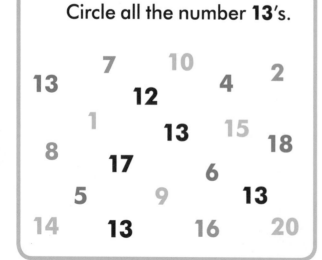

NUMBERS & COUNTING

14 Fourteen

Trace the number **14** and the word **fourteen**.

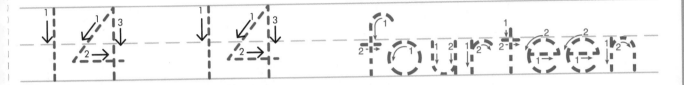

How many **ones** do you count?

How many **tens** do you count?

Count the deer and color the deer labeled number **14**.

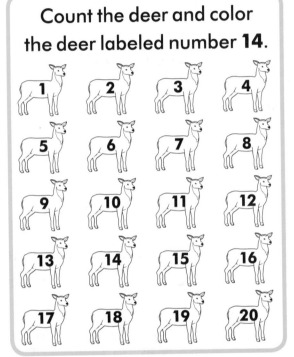

Circle all the number **14's**.

15   14   10
2   5
    7
  19   15
      3   8
14
    4   14
  18   1   6
20   12   16   14

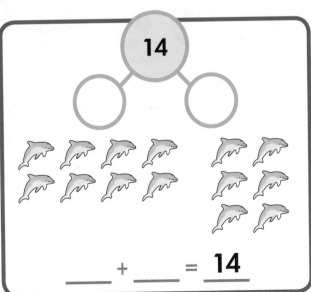

14

___ + ___ = **14**

☆10 ☆11 ☆12 ☆13 ☆14 ☆15 ☆16 ☆17 ☆18 ☆19 ☆20

Numbers

Tally marks are used to count or keep score. They are grouped in sets of five, which makes counting faster. Each | mark equals 1. After there are four | marks, a / mark crosses through them, which equals five.

1	I	6	||||| I
2	II	7	||||| II
3	III	8	||||| III
4	IIII	9	||||| IIII
5							10											

Count the tally marks and circle the correct number.

||||| ||||| |||

9   10   11
12   13   14

||||| ||||| ||||

9   10   11
12   13   14

· ·

Circle the eleventh heart.
Draw a line under the fourteenth heart.

· ·

Read the clues below. Draw a line from the clue to the correct answer.

7

The number is one greater than 2.

5

The number is one less than 9.

3

The number is one less than 6

8

14
12
10
8
6
4
2
⬆ ⬆

SKIP-COUNT BY
2's.

SAY THE NUMBERS OUT LOUD.

COLOR IN NUMBERS 13 AND 14

1 2 3 4 5 6 7 8 9

Numbers

Color the snowman with the **smallest number**.

Write the **smallest number**.

_____

Write the **largest number**.

_____

Fill in the missing numbers on the number lines below.

9   _____   11   _____

10   11   12   13   14   15   16   17   18   19   20

199

15 Fifteen

Trace the number **15** and the word **fifteen**.

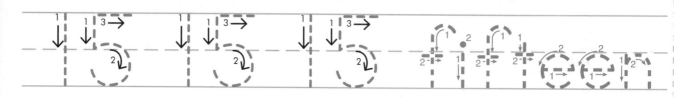

How many **ones** do you count?

How many **tens** do you count?

Count the acorns and color the acorn labeled number **15**.

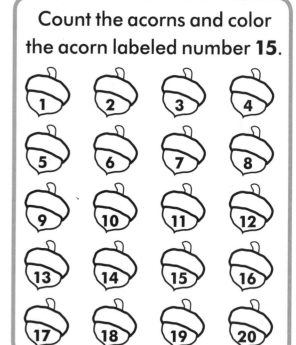

1 2 3 4
5 6 7 8
9 10 11 12
13 14 15 16
17 18 19 20

Circle all the number **15**'s.

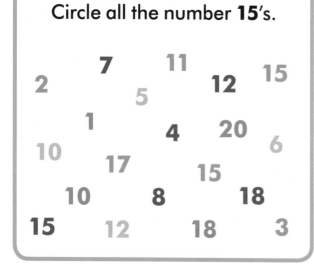

2   **7**   11   15
5   **12**
1   **4**   20   6
10
17   15
10   **8**   **18**
15   12   18   3

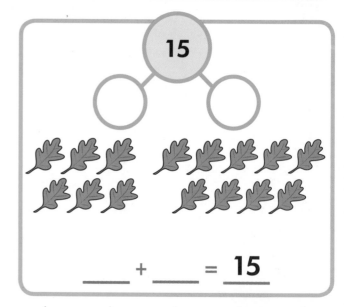

15

____ + ____ = **15**

COLOR IN NUMBERS 15 AND 16

1 2 3 4 5 6 7 8 9

200

NUMBERS & COUNTING

Numbers

16	13	15	6	7
5	16	14	9	15
15	13	8	13	15

_____ How many 13's do you see?

_____ How many 14's do you see?

_____ How many 15's do you see?

_____ How many 16's do you see?

Larger or Smaller

Color the lily pad with the smaller number **green**.

The **+** sign means you should add. Look at each of the groups below and count the number of animals. Write the correct number on the lines provided and then add the two numbers together to get the sum, or the total.

 _____ **+** 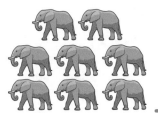 _____ **=** _____

 _____ **+** _____ **=** _____

⭐10 ⭐11 ⭐12 ⭐13 ⭐14 ⭐15 ⭐16 ⭐17 ⭐18 ⭐19 ⭐20

17 Seventeen

Trace the number **17** and the word **seventeen**.

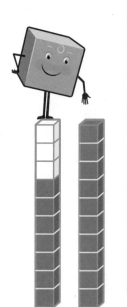

How many **ones** do you count?

How many **tens** do you count?

Count the drums and color the drum labeled number **17**.

1	2	3	4
5	6	7	8
9	10	11	12
13	14	15	16
17	18	19	20

Circle all the number **17**'s.

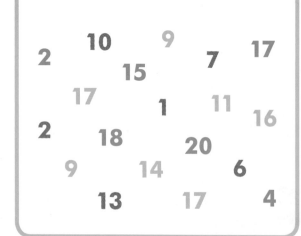

2   10   9   7   17
15
17   1   11
2   18   20   16
9   14   6
13   17   4

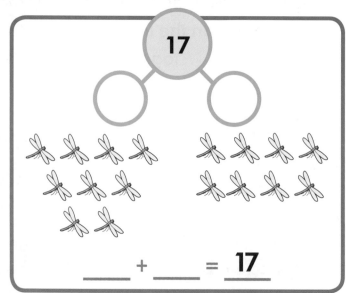

17

____ + ____ = **17**

NUMBERS & COUNTING

COLOR IN NUMBERS 17 AND 18

1 2 3 4 5 6 7 8 9

204

20 Twenty

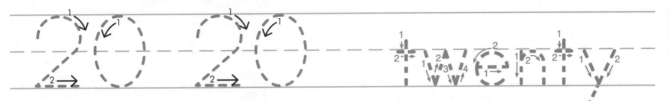

Trace the number **20** and the word **twenty**.

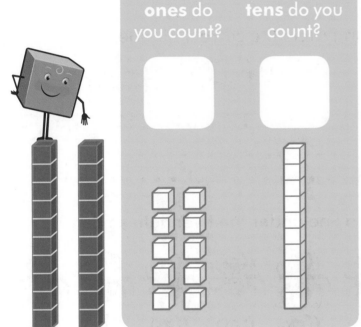

How many **ones** do you count?

How many **tens** do you count?

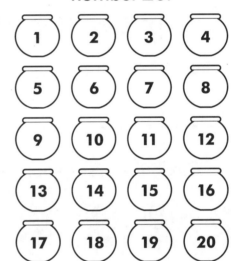

Count the fishbowls and color the fishbowl labeled number **20**.

1	2	3	4
5	6	7	8
9	10	11	12
13	14	15	16
17	18	19	20

Circle all the number **20**'s.

10   3
6   12   9
   20
15   1
20   5   14
   2
      16
13   8   20
4   18   11   19

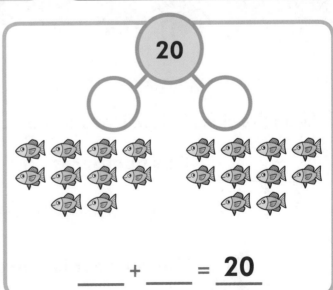

20

___ + ___ = **20**

☆10 ☆11 ☆12 ☆13 ☆14 ☆15 ☆16 ☆17 ☆18 ☆19 ☆20

Numbers

Tally marks are used to count or keep score. They are grouped in sets of five, which makes counting faster. Each | mark equals 1. After there are four | marks, a / mark crosses through them, which equals five.

1	I	6	⊞ I
2	II	7	⊞ II
3	III	8	⊞ III
4	IIII	9	⊞ IIII
5	⊞	10	⊞ ⊞

Count the tally marks and circle the correct number.

⊞ ⊞ ⊞ IIII   ⊞ ⊞ ⊞ ⊞

16 17 18 19 20   16 17 18 19 20

Circle the first spider. Draw a line under the twentieth spider.

Read the clues below. Draw a line from the clue to the correct answer.

17   This number is one greater than 18.   **18**

This number is one less than 19.

19   This number is one greater than 16.   **20**

COLOR IN NUMBERS 19 AND 20

Numbers

Help the bird get to her egg by following the numbers from **1** to **20** in order.

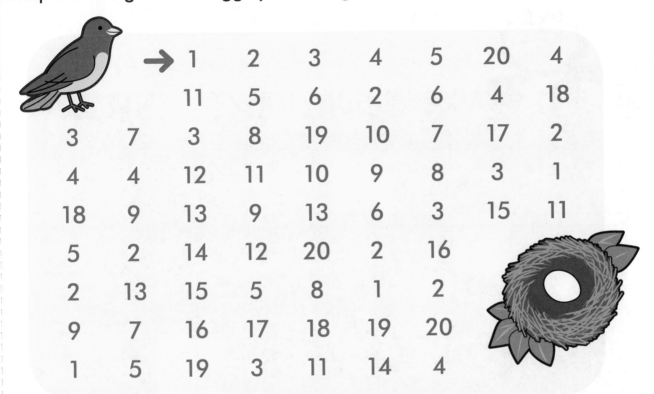

Skip-count by **2**'s, **3**'s, and **5**'s.

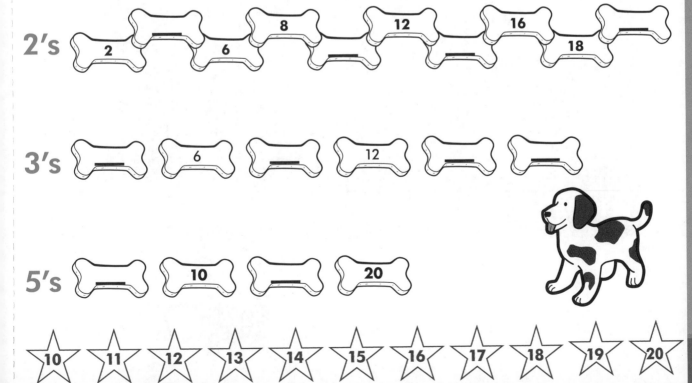

2's 2 6 8 12 16 18

3's 6 12

5's 10 20

10 11 12 13 14 15 16 17 18 19 20

Let's Count to 100!

Count up to 100, filling in the numbers that are missing.

1	2	3	4	5	6	7		9	10
11	12	13	14		16	17	18	19	20
21	22		24	25	26	27	28	29	30
31	32	33		35	36	37	38	39	40
41	42	43	44	45	46	47		49	50
51	52	53		55	56	57	58	59	60
61		63	64	65	66	67	68	69	70
71	72	73	74	75		77	78	79	80
81	82		84	85	86	87	88	89	90
91	92	93	94	95	96	97	98		100

COLORS & SHAPES

Yellow

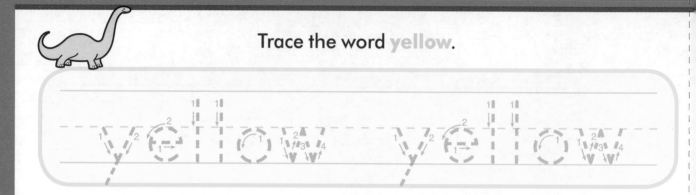

Trace the word yellow.

Help the yellow bees find their way to the hive.

Circle the yellow balloons.

Circle

A **circle** is round.
Practice drawing circles by tracing the circles below.

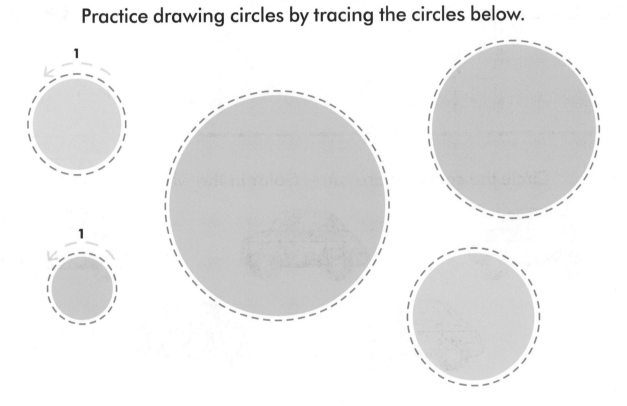

Trace the word **circle**.

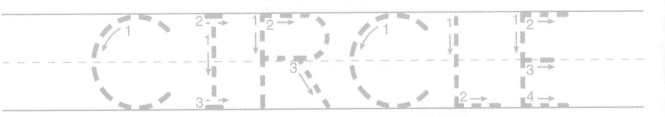

Color in the circles below yellow.

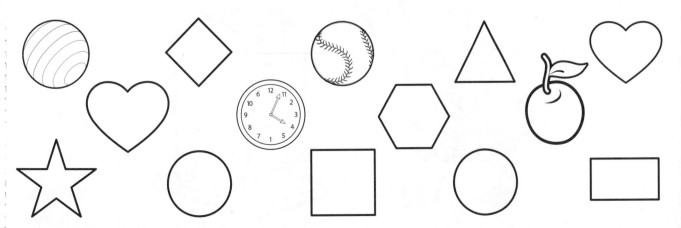

Blue

Trace the word **blue**.

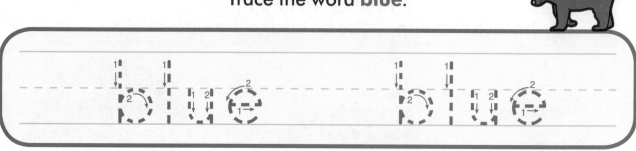

Circle the cars that are **blue**. Color in the white one **blue**.

Color the mail carrier's mailbox **blue**.

Square

A **square** has four sides of equal length.
Practice drawing **squares** by tracing the dotted lines below.

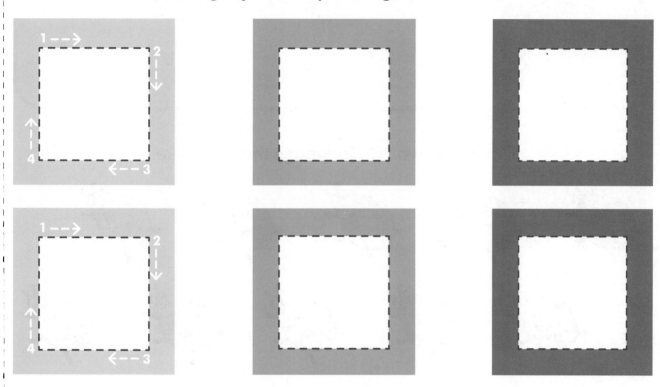

Trace the word **square**.

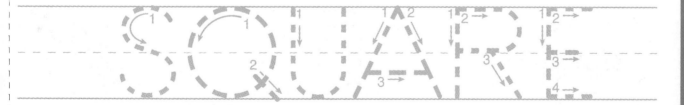

Trace the **squares** and color them **blue**.

Red

Trace the word **red**.

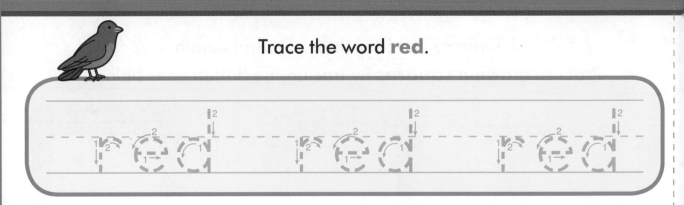

Circle the two **red** ladybugs that are alike.

Circle all of the foods that are **red**.

Heart

Practice drawing **hearts** by tracing the dotted lines below.

Trace the word **heart**.

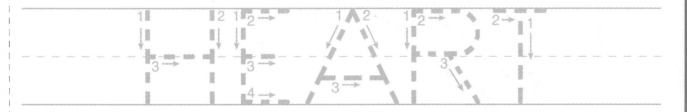

Trace the **hearts** below and then decorate the last cookie yourself.

Green

Trace the word **green**.

Connect the dots to find out what insect is **green** and then color it in.

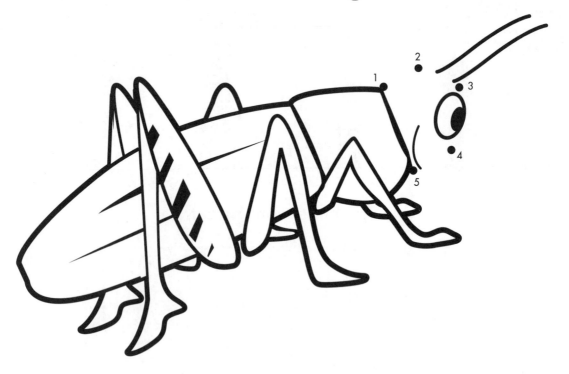

Circle all of the animals that are **green** below.

Rectangle

A **rectangle** has four sides. Two sides are long. Two sides are short. Practice drawing **rectangles** by tracing the dotted lines below.

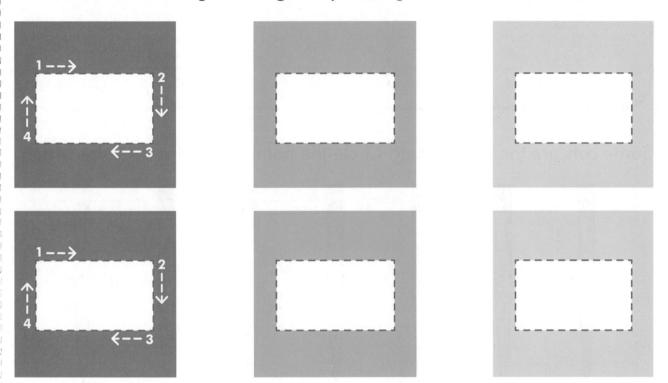

Trace the word **rectangle**.

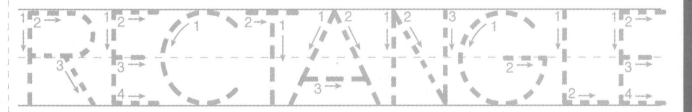

Trace the **rectangle**. Now color the train.

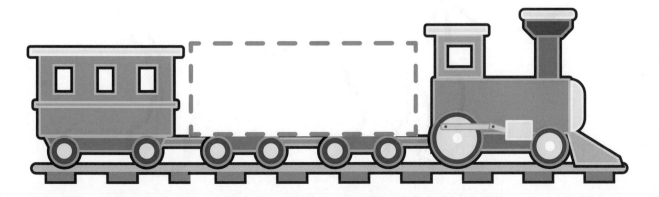

Black

Trace the word **black**.

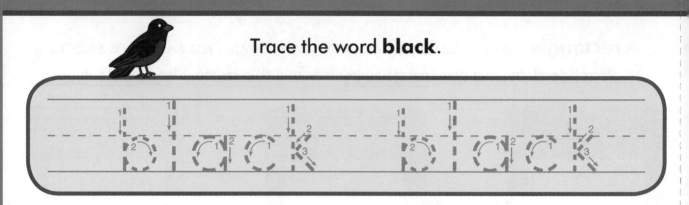

Some cats are the color **black**. Circle the paintbrush with the color **black**.

Now color the cat **black**.

Oval

Practice drawing **ovals** by tracing the **ovals** below.

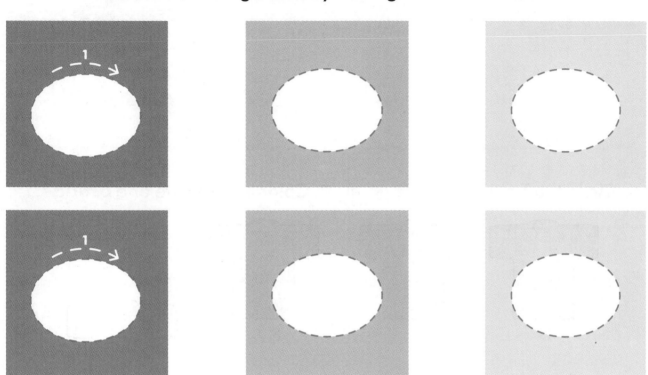

Trace the word **oval**.

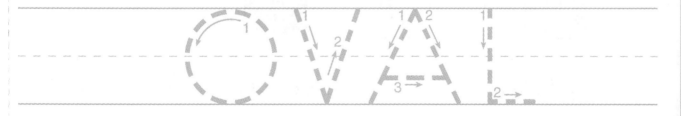

The spider has an **oval** body. Trace the oval and color it **black**.

COLORS & SHAPES

223

Orange

Trace the word orange.

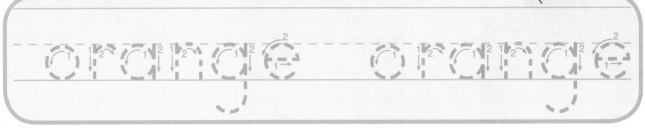

Circle the T-shirts that are orange. Color in the white one orange.

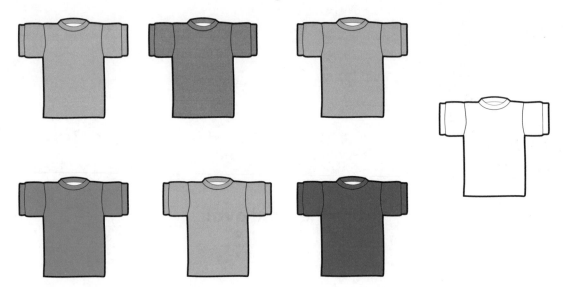

Circle the leaves that are orange. Color the white leaf orange.

Star

Trace the **stars**.

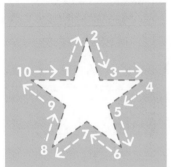  

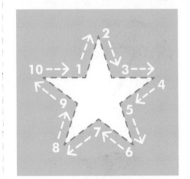 

Trace the word **star**.

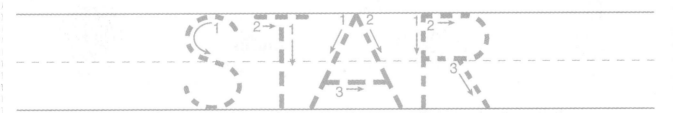

Color in the last **star** to complete the pattern.

Purple

Trace the word **purple**.

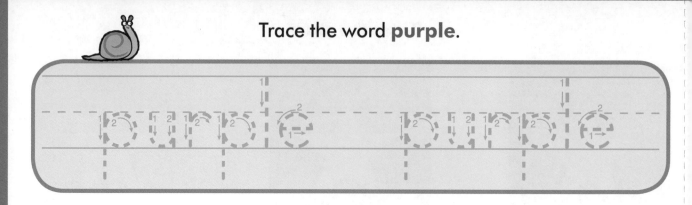

Circle everything that has **purple** in it below.

Violets are **purple** flowers. Color the violets below **purple**.

Triangle

A **triangle** has three sides.
Practice drawing triangles by tracing the triangles below.

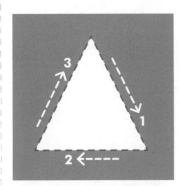

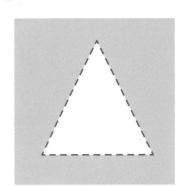
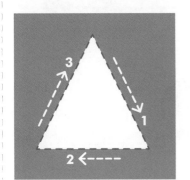
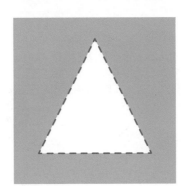
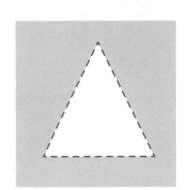

Trace the word **triangle**.

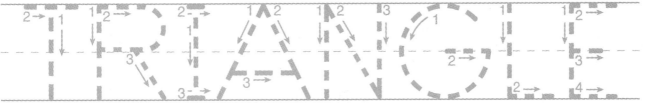

Color the seven **triangles** below **purple**.

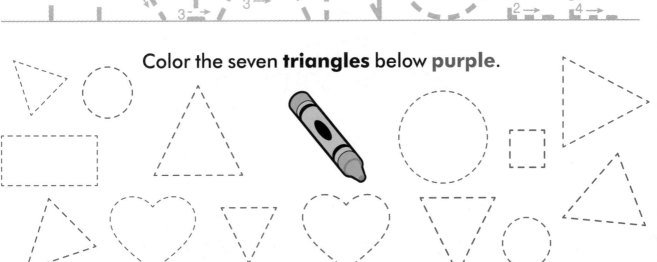

227

Pink

Trace the word **pink**.

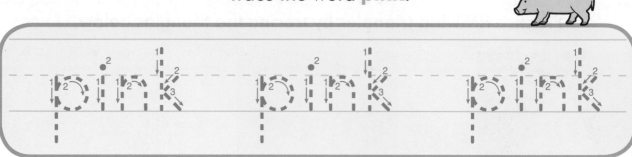

Circle all of the **pink** hearts.

Color the birthday cake **pink**.

Hungry Rabbit

Draw a line along the path that shows **orange** circles ⬤ and **green** triangles ▲ to help the rabbit find the carrot.

You Can Color

Let's get ready to paint. First, we need to add all the **colors** to the palette. Color them in.

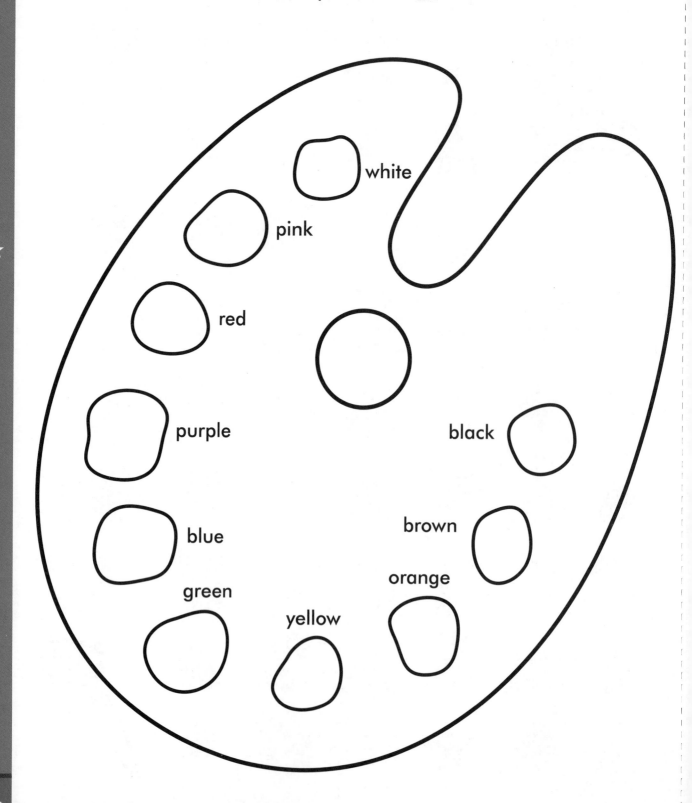

white

pink

red

purple

black

blue

brown

green

orange

yellow

Matching Hearts

Circle the **heart** that is the same as the first **heart** in each row.

Missing Colors

What colors are missing from the rainbow?
Color them in.

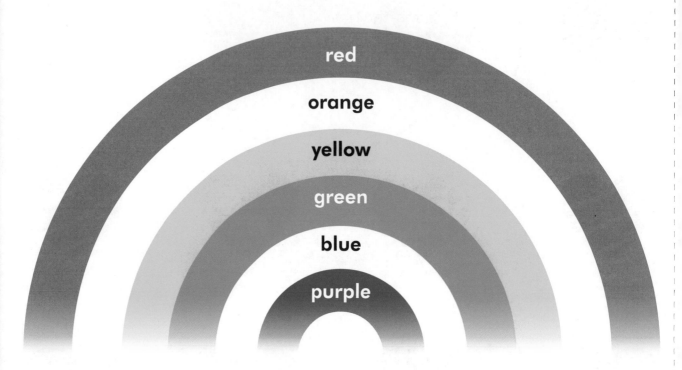

red

orange

yellow

green

blue

purple

Trace the color words below.

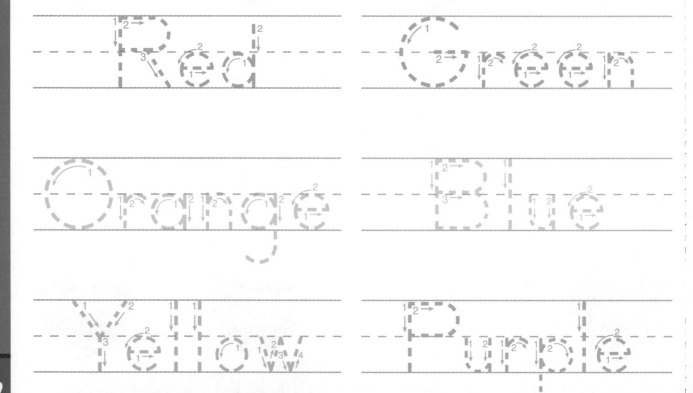

Find the Cheese

Draw a line along the path of *yellow* triangles ▲ and **blue** circles ● to lead the mouse to the cheese.

Playground Shapes

Find and circle the following shapes in the playground above.

circle

square

diamond

rectangle

triangle

oval

Pattern

Complete the pattern in each row by drawing and filling in a shape.

Shapes

Draw a line to match the animals to their shapes.
Then color them in!

3-D Shapes

Trace the names of the 3-D shapes below.

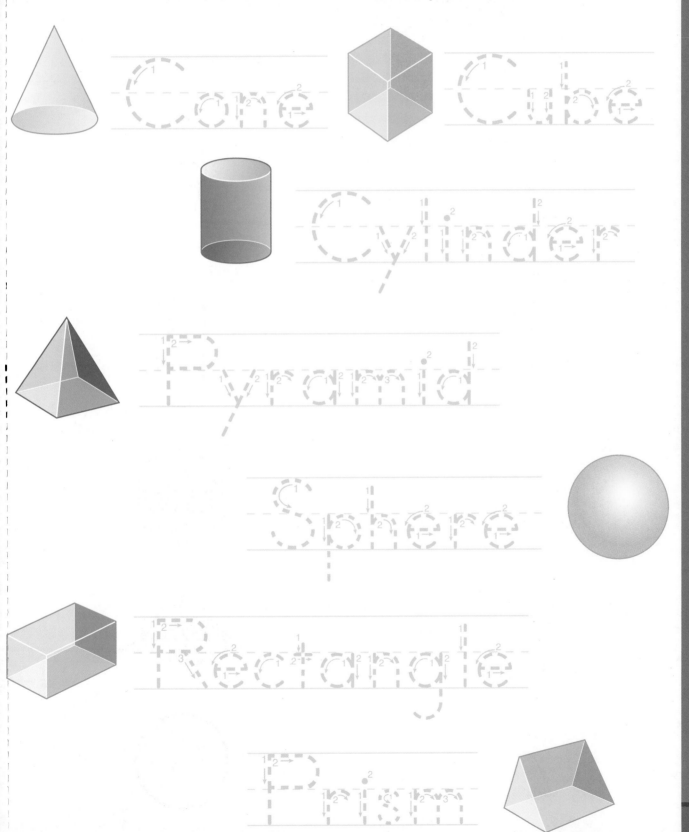

Cone

Cube

Cylinder

Pyramid

Sphere

Rectangle

Prism

3-D Shapes

Match each 3-D shape on the left to its real-life shape on the right.

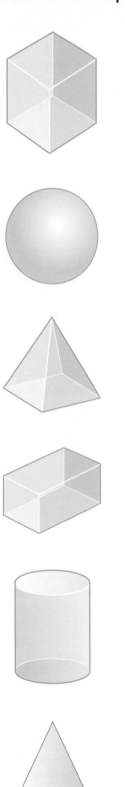

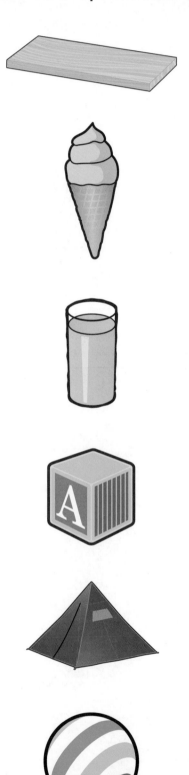

TIME & DATE

Telling Time

A clock shows twelve hours, which is half a day.
Fill in the missing hours.

Telling Time

minute hand
(long)

hour hand
(short)

Look at the hands on each clock.
Then color in the box with the correct time.

3:00

5:00

5:00

6:00

9:00

11:00

12:00

2:00

1:00

3:00

10:00

9:00

241

Telling Time

minute hand
(long)

hour hand
(short)

Look at the hands on each clock.
Then color in the box with the correct time.

2:00
5:00

12:00
8:00

7:00
4:00

6:00
8:00

10:00
5:00

11:00
7:00

What Time Is It?

Look at each of the clocks below. Write the correct time on the line provided. Remember, the short hand is the hour hand. The first one has been done for you.

_7_ :00

____ :00

____ :00

____ :00

____ :00

____ :00

____ :00

____ :00

____ :00

School Time
Draw the hands on the clock to show what time school begins.

TIME & DATE

243

What Time Is It?

Look at each of the times below. Draw the hour hands on the clocks to show the correct time. The first one has been done for you.

4:00

8:00

5:00

9:00

11:00

6:00

2:00

12:00

1:00

Sleep Time
Draw the hands on the clock to show your bedtime.

What Time Is It?

Look at the hands on each clock. Then draw a line to the box with its matching time. Remember, the small hand is the hour hand.

| 1:00 |
| 3:00 |
| 12:00 |

| 5:00 |
| 6:00 |
| 8:00 |

| 6:00 |
| 9:00 |
| 12:00 |

| 8:00 |
| 10:00 |
| 2:00 |

| 1:00 |
| 3:00 |
| 5:00 |

| 2:00 |
| 10:00 |
| 9:00 |

What Time Is It?

Look at the hands on each clock.
Then draw a line to the digital clock with its matching time.

7:00

8:00

5:00

11:00

3:00

2:00

246

What Time Is It?

Look at each of the clocks below. Write the correct time on the line provided. Remember, the small hand is the hour hand. The first one has been done for you.

__8__ :00

_____ :00

_____ :00

_____ :00

_____ :00

_____ :00

_____ :00

_____ :00

_____ :00

Lunchtime
Draw the hands on the clock to show what time you eat lunch.

What Time Is It?

Look at each of the times below. Draw the hour hands on the clocks to show the correct time. The first one has been done for you.

5:00

7:00

3:00

10:00

12:00

6:00

1:00

11:00

4:00

Playtime
Draw the hands on the clock to show a time when you play.

Days of the Week

Practice writing the days of the week.

Sunday   Monday   **Tuesday**   Wednesday

Thursday   **Friday**   Saturday

Circle what day it will be tomorrow.

Sunday   **Monday**   Tuesday   Wednesday

Thursday   Friday   Saturday

Days of the Week

Find the names of the days of the week in the word search puzzle below. The words go across, down, and diagonally.

Monday   Tuesday   Wednesday   Thursday
Friday   Saturday   Sunday

Y L M O N D A Y W X
W E D N E S D A Y V
N P M A X M Y P G S
E F A P R A L E H U
T U E S D A Y K C N
B U C I F I V M E D
E T R A G W E N M A
J F S A T U R D A Y
T H U R S D A Y E E

Circle what day it is today.

Sunday   Monday   Tuesday

Wednesday   Thursday   Friday

Saturday

Days of the Week

Solve the riddle below by filling in the
correct letter for each number.

1=A 2=B 3=C 4=D 5=E 6=F 7=G 8=H

9=I 10=J 11=K 12=L 13=M 14=N 15=O

16=P 17=Q 18=R 19=S 20=T 21=U

22=V 23=W 24=X 25=Y 26=Z

Name three days in a row without using the words Monday, Tuesday,
Wednesday, Thursday, Friday, Saturday, or Sunday.

___ ___ ___ ___ ___ ___ ___ ___ ___ ,
25 5   19 20 5   18 4   1   25

___ ___ ___ ___ ___ , and
20 15 4   1   25

___ ___ ___ ___ ___ ___ ___ ___ !
20 15 13 15 18 18 15 23

Circle what day it was yesterday.

Sunday   Monday   Tuesday   Wednesday

Thursday   Friday   Saturday

Months of the Year

There are twelve months in a year. Months are proper nouns and need to be **capitalized**.

January 1	February 2	March 3	April 4
May 5	June 6	July 7	August 8
September 9	October 10	November 11	December 12

What is the first month of the year?

_____

In what month is your birthday?

_____

In what month is the last day of school?

_____

What is the last month of the year?

_____

What month comes after April?

_____

Months of the Year

Look at the names of the months
and trace them in order.

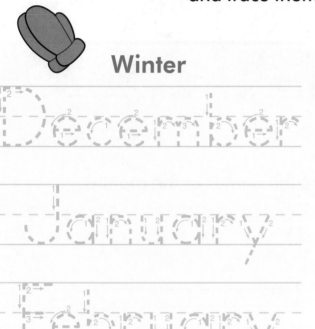

Winter

December

January

February

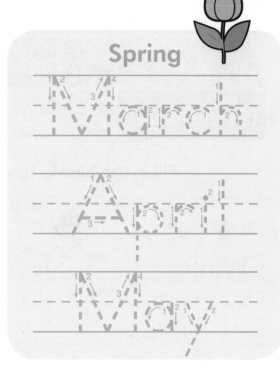

Spring

March

April

May

Summer

June

July

August

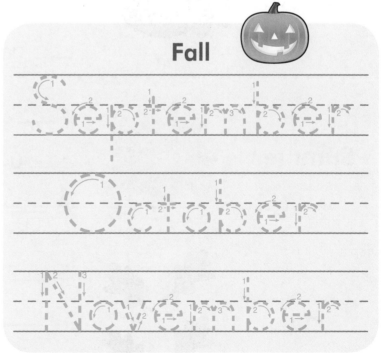

Fall

September

October

November

The four seasons are: **Winter** **Spring** **Summer** **Fall**

January	February	March	April
May	June	July	August
September	October	November	December

Fill in the blanks to write the names of the months.

Winter

D __ __ e m __ __ __

J __ __ __ __ __ __ __

__ e b __ __ __ __ __

Spring

M __ __ __ __ __

A __ __ __ __ __

__ a y

Summer

J __ __ e

__ u l __

A __ __ __ __ __ t

Fall

S __ p t __ __ __ __ __

O __ t __ __ __ __

__ __ v e m __ __ __

Fourth of July

The Fourth of July is a day to celebrate America's birthday.
It is the day we gained our independence from Britain.
Circle the symbol of America in each row that is different.

The flag of the United States is a symbol of freedom.
Color in the spaces with the letter **A red** and the
spaces with the letter **B blue** in the American flag below.

255

Halloween

Halloween is celebrated on October 31st.
Color the jack-o'-lantern below.

Use the alphabet code to solve the secret riddle.

A=1 B=2 C=3 D=4 E=5 F=6 G=7 H=8 I=9 J=10

K=11 L=12 M=13 N=14 O=15 P=16 Q=17 R=18

S=19 T=20 U=21 V=22 W=23 X=24 Y=25 Z=26

What was the favorite game at the ghosts' birthday party?

$\underline{}$ $\underline{}$ $\underline{}$ $\underline{}$ $\underline{}$ $\underline{}$ $\underline{}$
  8   9   4   5   1   14   4

$\underline{}$ $\underline{}$ $\underline{}$ $\underline{}$ $\underline{}$ $\underline{}$
  19   8   18   9   5   11

256

Thanksgiving

Thanksgiving is a day for giving thanks.
People give thanks for the all the good things that they have received during the year, and celebrate with feasting.

What are YOU thankful for this year?
Have your mom or dad help you write down what you are thankful for on the lines below.

- -

- -

- -

- -

- -

Happy Holidays

People celebrate many different holidays based on their beliefs. What holiday do you celebrate in December?

Draw a picture of a decoration used during the holiday.

Draw a picture of a special food you eat during the holiday.

Valentine's Day

Valentine's Day is celebrated on February 14th. Use the alphabet code to solve the secret message about Valentine's Day.

A=1 B=2 C=3 D=4 E=5 F=6 G=7 H=8

I=9 J=10 K=11 L=12 M=13 N=14 O=15

P=16 Q=17 R=18 S=19 T=20 U=21

V=22 W=23 X=24 Y=25 Z=26

___ ___ ___ ___   ___ ___ ___
23   9   12 12   25 15 21

___ ___   ___ ___
 2   5   13 25

___ ___ ___ ___ ___ ___ ___ ___ ___
22   1 12   5 14 20   9 14   5

Decorate the Valentine's Day cookies below.

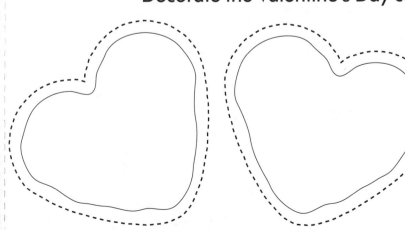
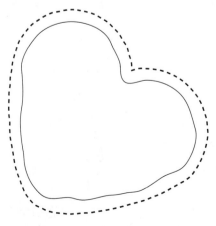

ME & MY WORLD

All About Me

Draw a picture of yourself using the outline below.
Look in the mirror first. What color eyes and hair do you have?
Is your skin light or dark? Do you have short hair or long?
What makes you you?

All About Me

This Is Me

My name is ....

I like to be called ....

My favorite food is ....

My favorite color is ....

My favorite sport is ....

My favorite book is ....

My favorite animal is ....

My favorite game is ....

My best friend's name is ....

All About Me

Fill in the information below
all about **you** and where you live.

My Name . . . .

My Street Address . . . .

. . . .

My City or Town . . . .

My State . . . .

My Country . . . .

I know my phone number!

_____ – _____ – _____

Use your fingers to dial your phone number.

When Is Your Birthday?

Circle the month and day of **your birthday**.

January	February	March	April
May	June	July	August
September	October	November	December

1	2	3	4	5	6	7	8
9	10	11	12	13	14	15	16
17	18	19	20	21	22	23	24
25	26	27	28	29	30	31	

Draw candles on the top of the cake—one for each year of your age. **Now decorate your cake!**

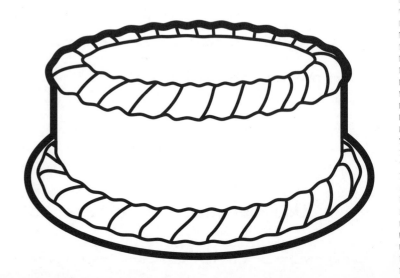

My Birthday

Fill in the blanks below.

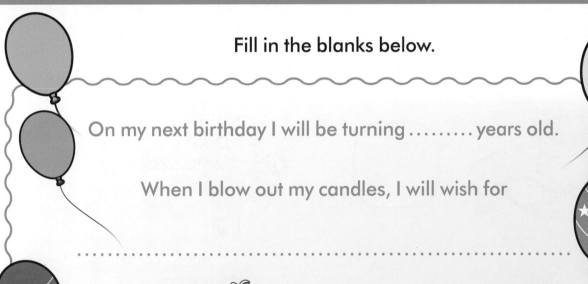

On my next birthday I will be turning .... years old.

When I blow out my candles, I will wish for

. . . .

The best 🎁 I ever got for a birthday was

. . . .

Find and circle the birthday party words from the word box in the word search below. The words may go across or down.

**BALLOONS   HAT   CAKE   CANDLES
ICE CREAM   GAMES   FRIENDS   PRESENTS**

W	C	F	I	C	E	C	R	E	A	M	H
B	A	L	L	O	O	N	S	Z	H	X	A
T	K	H	I	C	A	N	D	L	E	S	T
H	E	M	D	A	F	R	I	E	N	D	S
P	R	E	S	E	N	T	S	V	O	T	H
C	E	J	P	M	K	G	A	M	E	S	V

Morning and Night Routine

Look at the pictures below showing the boy getting ready in the morning. Write 1, 2, 3, and 4 to put them in the right order.

Look at the pictures below showing Zippy the Zebra getting ready to go to bed. Write 1, 2, 3, and 4 to put them in the right order.

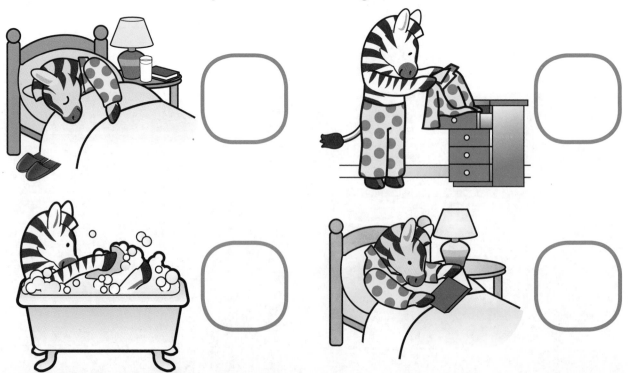

Exercise Is Fun!

Exercise is fun and keeps you healthy!
Exercise helps strengthen your bones and muscles and keeps
your heart healthy. There are many ways to exercise that are fun
as long as you keep active or moving! Look at the pictures below.
Circle **active** or **not active** under each picture.

Active   Not Active

Active   Not Active

Active   Not Active

Active   Not Active

Active   Not Active

Active   Not Active

Active   Not Active

Active   Not Active

Hand Washing

There are germs on your hands. They are so small you can't see them. Germs can make you sick. If you wash your hands, that kills the germs. Color in the germs.

Put the following steps for washing hands in the correct order by putting 1 to 5 in the circles.

1 Wet hands   **2** Use soap   **3** Lather, rub, and count to 20

4 Rinse   **5** Dry off hands with a towel

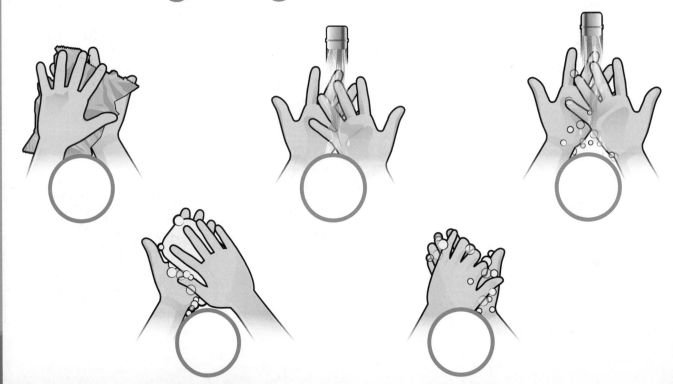

Your Teeth

How many teeth do I have? Count them.

I have _____ upper teeth. I have _____ lower teeth.

I have _____ teeth altogether.

Brush your teeth every morning and night to keep them healthy and clean. Put a number from 1 to 5 in each box to show the correct order in brushing your teeth. Flossing each day also removes food the toothbrush missed.

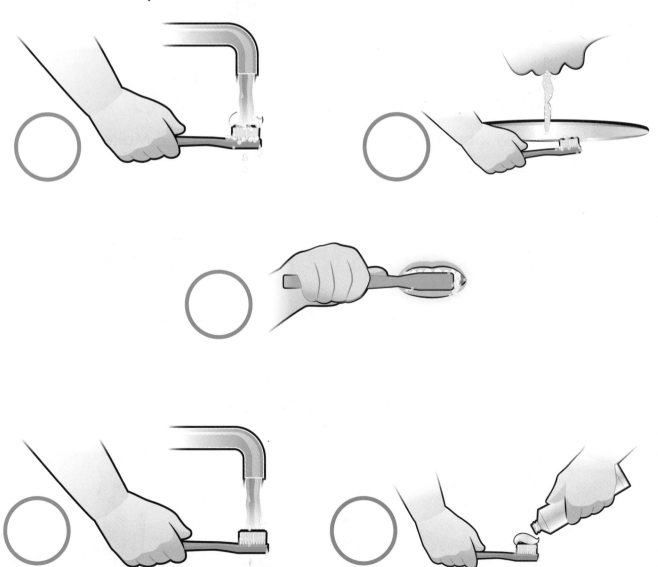

Tying Your Shoes

Tying Your Shoe: The **Bunny Ears** Method

1

2

Steps 1 & 2 First make a knot for the bunny's head.
Take the laces and cross them over to make an "X."
Then, pull one lace through the bottom of the "X" and pull tight.

3

4

Step 3 Now loop the laces into bunny ears.

Step 4 Make an "X" using the bunny ears.

5

6

Step 5 Slide one ear under the "X."

Step 6 Pull tightly.

Circle the picture that happened **before** Claire put on her shoes.

Family Members

Trace the names of family members below.

How many people are in your family? _____.

Do you have any brothers?

YES   NO

If so, how many? _____

Do you have any sisters?

YES   NO

If so, how many? _____

Draw your family in the house below.

Family Traditions

A family tradition is something a family does together over and over that is meaningful to them.

Family traditions might be as simple as making the same peppermint cookies every Christmas, pizza night Fridays, or visiting the same cabin in Maine every summer.

Family traditions might have started years ago with your grandparents or last month with your family.

Think about a **tradition** in your family.
Draw a picture of it in the box below.

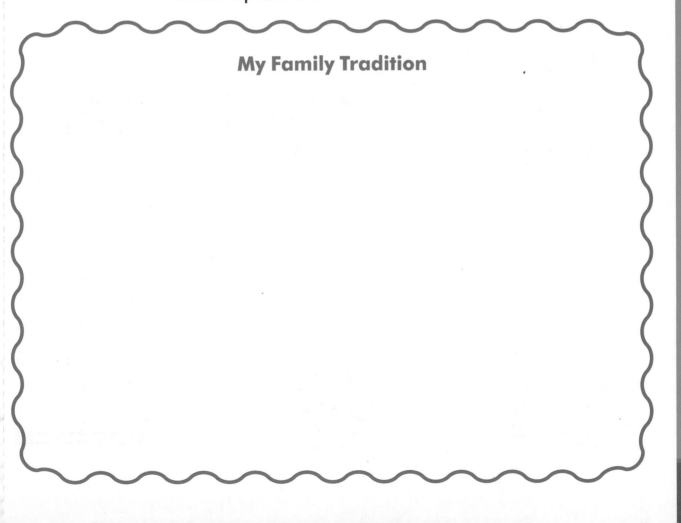

My Family Tradition

Pets

Do you have a **pet**? If so, circle it below.
If not, circle one you'd like to have.

Car Safety

Whenever you ride in a car, you must sit in the back seat and wear your seat belt. Circle the picture below showing the right way to ride in a car.

Helmets

Helmets are important for safety.
Draw a line from the boy with the **helmet** to
activities where he must wear a **helmet**.

**playing
basketball**

**riding a
scooter**

**riding in
a car**

**riding a
skateboard**

**going to
the dentist**

**riding a
bike**

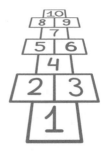

**playing
hopscotch**

Crossing the Street

**Before you cross a street,
Stop, Look, and Listen!**

Draw a line from each word
to its matching picture.

STOP

LOOK

LISTEN

Draw a line between the traffic light color and what it means.

GO   STOP   SLOW

277

Places in My Neighborhood

A **neighborhood** is an area of a town or city where people live. Besides many different types of homes, there are a lot of different businesses there, too. Look at each place and then circle the object that goes with it.

People in My Neighborhood

There are many helpful people in your **neighborhood**. Match the helpers below with the object that goes with each one. Circle the correct answer.

What would you like to do when you grow up?

NATURE & SCIENCE

Feather, Fur, or Scales

All animals have special traits that make them different from one another, such as having feathers, fur, or scales.
Put the animals in the group where they belong.

Draw a square ■ around all animals with feathers.

Draw a circle ● around all animals with scales.

Draw a triangle ▲ around all animals with fur.

NATURE & SCIENCE

285

Animal Habitats: Forest

A **habitat** is where an animal lives. There are many different **habitats**. One **habitat** is the forest. Circle what animals would live in the forest.

Animal Habitats: Savanna

A **savanna** is a hot, dry grassland found in places like Africa, Australia, and Madagascar. Circle what animals would live in the **savanna**.

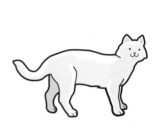

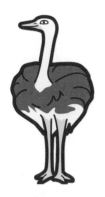

287

Animal Habitats: Ocean

Another animal **habitat** is the ocean. Circle all of the animals that you would find in the ocean.

What Do Plants Need?

Plants need soil to grow. It provides nutrients, which is the plants' food.

Plants need sunlight for photosynthesis, which changes the nutrients in soil into energy to grow.

Water provides nutrients for the plants and helps break those nutrients down in the soil.

Label the pictures in order of 1 to 4 to show how a plant grows.

The Life Cycle of a Butterfly

1   First, an egg is laid on a leaf, and a caterpillar is born from that egg.

2   The caterpillar spends most of its life eating leaves.

3   When it gets big enough, the caterpillar attaches itself to a twig and forms a chrysalis, or a cocoon.

4   Hatching out of the chrysalis is a beautiful butterfly! Color the butterfly below.

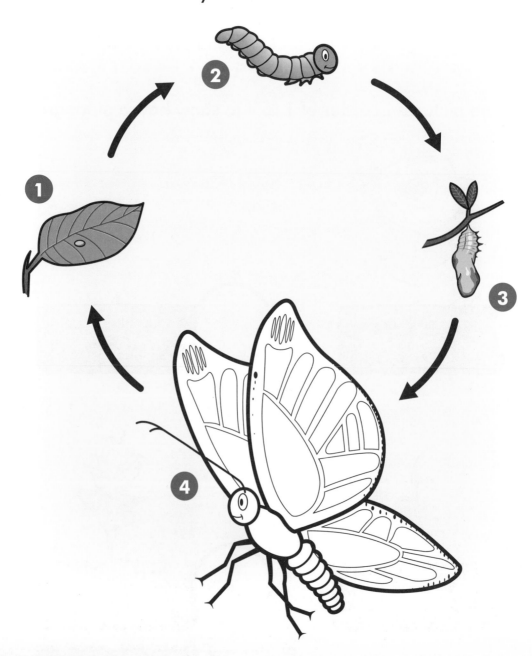

Living or Nonliving

The world is made up of both living and nonliving things.
All living things grow, reproduce, and need food, air, and water.
Circle anything below that is living.

Weather

Draw a line connecting the **weather** to its name.

Sun

Rain

Wind

Snow

hot

cold

The Four Seasons

Winter occurs in three months:
December   January   February
Below is a farm in **winter**.

Circle the words that
describe the weather
in **winter**.

Rainy   Hot

Windy   Cold

Snowy   Cool

Spring occurs in three months:
March   April   May
Below is a farm in **spring**.

Circle the words that
describe the weather
in **spring**.

Rainy   Hot

Windy   Cold

Snowy   Cool

The Four Seasons

Summer occurs in three months:
June   July   August
Below is a farm in **summer**.

Circle the words that
describe the weather
in **summer**.

Rainy   Hot

Windy   Cold

Snowy   Cool

Fall occurs in three months:
September   October   November
Below is a farm in **fall**.

Circle the words that
describe the weather
in **fall**.

Rainy   Hot

Windy   Cold

Snowy   Cool

The Four Seasons

Trace the season words. Then decorate each tree
based on how you think it would look in that season.

Earth Day Every Day

Earth Day is on April 22nd every year. **Earth Day** reminds us to take care of our planet by keeping it clean. Yet we should be doing that every day! We can do that with by practicing a policy of **reduce**, **reuse**, and **recycle**.

Reduce

Reuse

Recycle

Reduce means to use less of something, such as water.

Reuse means to use things again, instead of just throwing them away.

Recycle means to make something new from something old. We recycle bottles to make new bottles.

Look at the definitions above. Think of one example for each of how we can **reduce**, **reuse**, and **recycle**. Draw a picture of your examples in the boxes below.

Color in the 3 **R**'s sign below. What color? Green, of course!

Earth Day Every Day

Reduce, Reuse, Recycle
(Sung to "Eensy Weensy Spider")

Reduce, Reuse, Recycle—words that we all know.
We have to save our planet so we can live and grow.
We might be only small children, but we will try, you'll see.
And we can save this planet—it starts with you and me!

Help sort the garbage.
Draw a line from each item to either
the trash can or the recycling bin.

The Three States of Matter: Solid, Liquid, and Gas

Solid is a type of matter.

A **solid** takes up space.
It has its own shape and size.
Color all of the **solids** below.

The Three States of Matter: Solid, Liquid, and Gas

Liquid is a type of matter.

It does not have its own shape.
It takes the shape of the container it is in.
Color all of the **liquids** below.

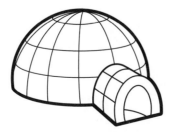

The Three States of Matter: Solid, Liquid, and Gas

Gas is a type of matter.

It does not have its own shape.
Circle all of the **gases** below.

The Five Senses: Smell

We use our nose to **smell**.

Draw a circle around everything that **smells** good.

We use our ears  to **hear**.

Draw something you would **hear** at the zoo.

The Five Senses: Taste

We use our mouth to **taste**.

Color in the items that you would **taste** on a farm.

 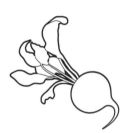 

The Five Senses: Sight

We use our eyes 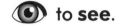 to **see**.

Look in a mirror. Draw what you **see**

The Five Senses: Touch

We use our hands  to **touch**.

Things can feel smooth, rough, soft, or hard to the touch.
Circle anything that is soft.

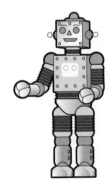

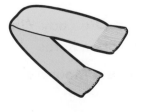

305

SUGGESTED READING

ABC, I Like Me! by Nancy Carlson

Alphabet Under Construction by Denise Fleming

Amelia Bedelia by Peggy Parish

Antics: An Alphabet Anthology by Catherine Hepworth

Are You My Mother? by Philip Eastman

The Art Lesson by Tomie De Paola

Bear Wants More by Karma Wilson

Blueberries for Sal by Robert McCloskey

The Cat in the Hat by Dr. Seuss

Click, Clack, Moo: Cows That Type by Doreen Cronin

Clifford the Big Red Dog by Norman Bridwell

Curious George by Han Augusto Rey

Don't Let the Pigeon Drive the Bus by Mo Willems

Down by the Bay by Raffi

Eensy, Weensy, Spider by May Ann Hoberman

Five Little Monkeys by Eileen Christelow

Frog and Toad Are Friends by Arnold Lobel

George and Martha by James Marshall

A Giraffe and a Half by Shel Silverstein

Green Eggs and Ham by Dr. Seuss

Harold and the Purple Crayon by Crockket Johnson

How Many? How Much? by Rosemary Wells

I Know an Old Lady Who Swallowed a Fly by Brian Karas

If You Give a Mouse a Cookie by Laura Joffe Numeroff

Is It Red? Is It Yellow? Is It Blue? by Tana Hoban

Lilly's Purple Plastic Purse by Kevin Henkes

The Little Engine That Could by Watty Piper

Madeline by Ludwig Bemelmans

Make Way for Ducklings by Robert McCloskey

Math Curse by Jon Scieszka

Miss Bindergarten Gets Ready for Kindergarten (series) by Joseph Slate

No, David! by David Shannon

Olivia by Ian Falconer

One Fish, Two Fish, Red Fish, Blue Fish by Dr. Seuss

One Hungry Monster by Susan Heyboer O'Keefe

The Polar Express by Chris Van Allsburg

Read-Aloud Rhymes for the Very Young by Jack Prelutsky

Red Leaf, Yellow Leaf by Lois Elhert

The Snowy Day by Ezra Jack Keats

The Story of Ferdinand by Munro Leaf

Strega Nona by Tomie de Paola

Sylvester and the Magic Pebble by William Steig

Two Little Trains by Margaret Wise Brown

The Velveteen Rabbit by Margery Williams

What Do You Do With a Tail Like This? by Steve Jenkins

Where the Wild Things Are by Maurice Sendak

ANSWER KEY

Page 10

Uppercase Letter A

Page 13
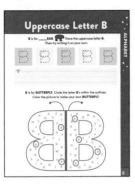
Uppercase Letter B

Page 14
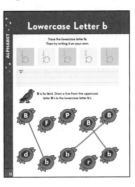
Lowercase Letter b

Page 15

Beginning Sounds

Page 17

Lowercase Letter c

Page 18

Beginning Sounds

Page 20
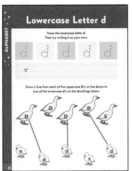
Lowercase Letter d

Page 21

Beginning Sounds

Page 22

Uppercase Letter E

Page 23
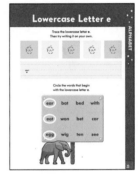
Lowercase Letter e

Page 24

Beginning Sounds

Page 25

Uppercase Letter F

Page 26
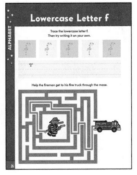
Lowercase Letter f

Page 29

Lowercase Letter g

Page 30

Beginning Sounds

Page 31

Uppercase Letter H

Page 32

Lowercase Letter h

Page 33

Beginning Sounds

Page 34
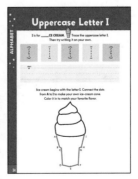
Uppercase Letter I

Page 35

Lowercase Letter i

ANSWER KEY

Page 36

Page 38
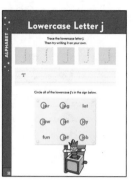

Page 39

Page 40

Page 41

Page 42

Page 44

Page 45
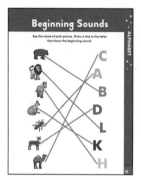

Page 46

Page 47
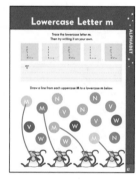

Page 49
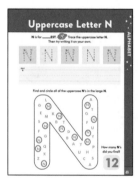

Page 51

Page 52

Page 53

Page 54

Page 56
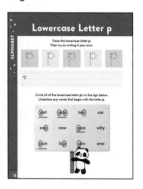

Page 57

Page 58

Page 59
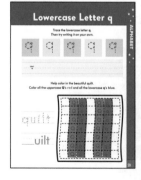

Page 60
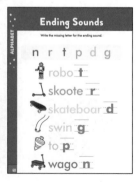

Page 61

Uppercase Letter R

Page 62

Lowercase Letter r

Page 64

Uppercase Letter S

Page 65

Lowercase Letter s

Page 66

Beginning Sounds

Page 68

Lowercase Letter t

Page 69

Beginning Sounds

Page 70

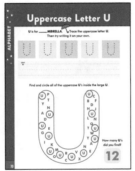

Uppercase Letter U

Page 71

Lowercase Letter u

Page 72

Beginning Sounds

Page 73

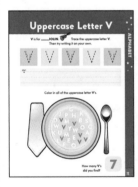

Uppercase Letter V

Page 74

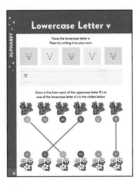

Lowercase Letter v

Page 75

Beginning Sounds

Page 77

Lowercase Letter w

Page 78

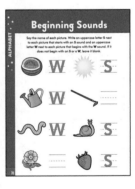

Beginning Sounds

Page 79

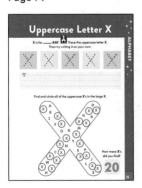

Uppercase Letter X

Page 80

Lowercase Letter x

Page 81

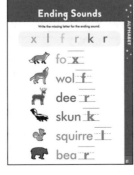

Ending Sounds

Page 82

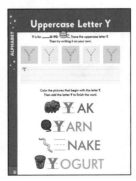

Uppercase Letter Y

Page 83

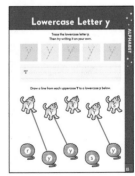

Lowercase Letter y

ANSWER KEY

Page 84

Beginning Sounds

Say the name of each picture. Circle the picture that begins with the sound of the letter in each row.

Kk | Ll | Mm | Nn | Oo | Pp

Page 85

Uppercase Letter Z

Z is for ZEBRA. Trace the uppercase letter Z. Then try writing it on your own.

Find and circle all of the uppercase Z's hidden at the ZOO.

How many Z's did you find? **7**

Page 88

Sight Word: AM

Trace the sight word on the dotted lines. Write it to complete the sentence.

am / AM

I **am** excited to go to the zoo today!

Color the boxes with the word am.

	in	are
all		at
is		as

Page 89

Sight Word: WITH

Trace the sight word on the dotted lines. Write it to complete the sentence.

with / WITH

I like to play tag **with** my best friend.

Find the words AM and WITH two times in the word search below. The words may go across or down.

W P E F D I D A F L
I J U A M D V M B K
T T K H K I B F N O
H O E M Y W I T H R

Page 90

Sight Word: ARE

Trace the sight word on the dotted lines. Write it to complete the sentence.

are / ARE

They **are** waiting for the bus.

Color the stars with the word are in them.

Page 91

Sight Word: AT

Trace the sight word on the dotted lines. Write it to complete the sentence.

at / AT

We had fun **at** the party!

Circle the sight words are and at in the sentences below.

We **are** at the park.
Are you going to join us?
Meet up **at** 12:00.

Page 92

Sight Word: RAN

Trace the sight word on the dotted lines. Write it to complete the sentence.

ran / RAN

I **ran** all the way home.

Find the words GET and RAN two times in the word search below. The words may go across or down.

R Y F H R W G A N
G E T K A X E F P
C M D Q N B T D L
X O R E M U R A N

Page 93

Sight Word: GET

Trace the sight word on the dotted lines. Write it to complete the sentence.

get / GET

May we please **get** some ice cream?

Color the boxes with the word get.

go	bet
got		set
met	let	but

Page 94

Sight Words: DID

Trace the sight word on the dotted lines. Write it to complete the sentence.

did / DID

Did you have fun at the playground?

Find the words CAME and DID two times in the word search below. The words may go across or down.

D I D U P E F D C C
J D V W J U L I Q A
K C A M E K H D J M
Y P S V O E M I N E

Page 95

Sight Word: CAME

Trace the sight word on the dotted lines. Write it to complete the sentence.

came / CAME

I'm glad the sun **came** out!

Color the diamonds with the word came in them.

Page 96

Sight Word: DO

Trace the sight word on the dotted lines. Write it to complete the sentence.

do / DO

What vegetables **do** you like to eat?

Circle the sight words same and do in the sentences below.

We **came** to play and have fun.
What **do** you like to **do** for fun?
Do you like to dance?

Page 97

Sight Word: EAT

Trace the sight word on the dotted lines. Write it to complete the sentence.

eat / EAT

I love to **eat** pizza!

Color the word eat.

eat

Page 98

Sight Word: SAY

Trace the sight word on the dotted lines. Write it to complete the sentence.

say / SAY

Say thank-you when someone gives you a present.

Color the boxes with the word say in them.

sat	say	are
day	may	out
say	see	hay

Page 99

Sight Word: GOOD

Trace the sight word on the dotted lines. Write it to complete the sentence.

good / GOOD

Exercise is **good** for you!

Find the words SAY and GOOD two times in the word search below. The words may go across or down.

I D U P E F G D C L
D G O O D L O I Q B
I A J T K H O S A Y
I S A Y E M D I N Y

Page 100

Sight Word: HAVE

Trace the sight word on the dotted lines. Write it to complete the sentence.

have / HAVE

I **have** to take a bath.

Color the hearts with the word have in them.

Page 101

Sight Word: HE

Trace the sight word on the dotted lines. Write it to complete the sentence.

he / HE

He is strong!

Circle the sight words have and he in the sentences below.

I **have** a little brother.
He is three years old.
He and I **have** a lot of fun together.

Page 102

Sight Word: INTO

Trace the sight word on the dotted lines. Write it to complete the sentence.

into / INTO

The pig fell **into** the mud.

Color the word into.

into

Page 103

Sight Word: LIKE

Trace the sight word on the dotted lines. Write it to complete the sentence.

like / LIKE

Do you **like** clowns?

Find the words INTO and LIKE two times in the word search below. The words may go across or down.

B Q L I K E I K L
H G B C K N W I
V J N M A L T R K
I N T O R E O E E

Page 104

Sight Word: NEW

Trace the sight word on the dotted lines. Write it to complete the sentence.

new / NEW

I got a **new** kite for my birthday!

Find the words WILL and NEW two times in the word search below. The words may go across or down.

W P E F N E W L D A
J I N L O I Q B Z
L T E H O G E T G X
L T W M D I W I L L

Page 105

Sight Word: WILL

Trace the sight word on the dotted lines. Write it to complete the sentence.

will / WILL

Will you share your cookie with me?

Color each of the circles with the word will in them.

ANSWER KEY

Page 106

Sight Word: NOW
Trace the sight word on the dotted lines.
Write it to complete the sentence.

now
NOW

Please do your homework right **now**.

| now | now | saw |

Circle the sight words **will** and **now** in the sentences below.

Will you come here right **now**?

We **will** be leaving soon.

Now it is time to go.

Page 107

Sight Word: ON
Trace the sight word on the dotted lines.
Write it to complete the sentence.

on
ON

The hamster ran **on** the wheel.

| on | on | on |

Color the word **on**.

on

Page 108

Sight Word: MUST
Trace the sight word on the dotted lines.
Write it to complete the sentence.

must
MUST

To be a good artist, you **must** paint every day!

| must | must | must |

Color the boxes with the word **must** in them.

mom	must	most
must	more	much
might	dust	must

Page 109

Sight Word: PLEASE
Trace the sight word on the dotted lines.
Write it to complete the sentence.

please
PLEASE

Please read me a book.

| please | please | please |

Find the words **MUST** and **PLEASE** two times in the word search below.
The words may go across or down.

G	U	W	M	T	I	M	S	T	M
L	E	F	P	L	E	A	S	E	U
M	U	S	T	I	Q	L	Z	K	S
P	L	E	A	S	E	G	X	P	T

Page 110

Sight Word: PRETTY
Trace the sight word on the dotted lines.
Write it to complete the sentence.

pretty
PRETTY

That dress is so **pretty**!

| pretty | pretty | pretty |

Color the squares with the word **pretty** in them.

pretty	party	please	really
	pass	silly	pretty
	pretty	pity	

Page 111

Sight Word: SAW
Trace the sight word on the dotted lines.
Write it to complete the sentence.

saw
SAW

I **saw** the White House in Washington, D.C.

| saw | saw | saw |

Circle the sight words **pretty** and **saw** in the sentences below.

I **saw** a pretty ladybug sitting on a leaf.

It had six **pretty** spots.

When it **saw** me, it flew away.

Page 112

Sight Word: RIDE
Trace the sight word on the dotted lines.
Write it to complete the sentence.

ride
RIDE

I like to **ride** my bike.

| ride | ride | ride |

Color the word **ride**.

ride

Page 113

Sight Word: WENT
Trace the sight word on the dotted lines.
Write it to complete the sentence.

went
WENT

I **went** to the grocery store with my mom.

| went | went | went |

Find the words **EAT** and **WENT** two times in the word search below.
The words may go across or down.

D	F	E	A	T	B	W	R	J
Y	C	K	V	G	O	E	A	T
W	E	N	T	J	E	N	Y	M
C	R	E	Z	I	V	T	B	A

Page 114

Sight Word: SHE
Trace the sight word on the dotted lines.
Write it to complete the sentence.

she
SHE

She is my best friend!!

| she | she | she |

Find the words **WHO** and **SHE** two times in the word search below.
The words may go across or down.

W	F	S	M	R	T	C	Z	K	P
H	U	H	H	X	E	S	A	Y	T
O	E	E	L	G	K	U	W	H	O
W	M	E	G	X	S	H	E	R	W

Page 115

Sight Word: WHO
Trace the sight word on the dotted lines.
Write it to complete the sentence.

who
WHO

Who is your teacher?

| who | who | who |

Color the triangles with the word **who** in them.

who · what · how · who
when · who · war
was · wet

Page 116
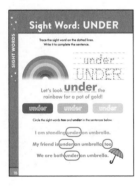
Sight Word: UNDER
Trace the sight word on the dotted lines.
Write it to complete the sentence.

under
UNDER

Let's look **under** the rainbow for a pot of gold!

| under | under | under |

Circle the sight words **too** and **under** in the sentences below.

I am standing **under** an umbrella.

My friend is **under** an umbrella **too**.

We are both **under** an umbrella.

Page 117

Sight Word: THAT
Trace the sight word on the dotted lines.
Write it to complete the sentence.

that
THAT

That koala is in a tree.

| that | that | that |

Color the word **that**.

that

Page 118

Sight Word: BUT
Trace the sight word on the dotted lines.
Write it to complete the sentence.

but
BUT

I like baseball, **but** soccer is my favorite sport.

| but | but | but |

Color the boxes with the word **but**.

bun	but	out
but	bin	bat
hut	rut	but

Page 119

Sight Word: THIS
Trace the sight word on the dotted lines.
Write it to complete the sentence.

this
THIS

This is my pet fish, Goldie.

| this | this | this |

Find the words **BUT** and **THIS** two times in the word search below.
The words may go across or down.

T	X	S	H	E	T	H	I	S	M
B	T	H	B	U	T	H	U	E	H
E	B	A	Y	T	Y	I	Q	L	
T	K	T	H	I	S	W	M	S	G

Page 120

Sight Word: TOO
Trace the sight word on the dotted lines.
Write it to complete the sentence.

too
TOO

I like to play in the rain, **too**!

| too | too | too |

Color the stars with the word **too** in them.

too · ten · moo
too · two
tot · too

Page 121

Sight Word: SOON
Trace the sight word on the dotted lines.
Write it to complete the sentence.

soon
SOON

Soon it will be winter!

| soon | soon | soon |

Circle the sight words **who** and **soon** in the sentences below.

Soon I will leave for camp.

I wonder **who** comes next.

Who will be in my cabin?

Page 122

Sight Word: WANT
Trace the sight word on the dotted lines.
Write it to complete the sentence.

want
WANT

I **want** to find a secret treasure!

| want | want | want |

Color the word **want**.

want

Page 123

Sight Word: OUR
Trace the sight word on the dotted lines.
Write it to complete the sentence.

our
OUR

This is **our** mail carrier.

| our | our | our |

Find the words **WANT** and **OUR** two times in the word search below.
The words may go across or down.

O	H	A	O	N	K	Y	W	Z
U	C	P	H	R	W	A	N	T
R	B	R	J	T	E	K	R	L
K	W	A	N	T	O	U	R	

Page 124

Sight Word: NO
Trace the sight word on the dotted lines.
Write it to complete the sentence.

no
NO

No, I do not like snakes.

| no | no | no |

Find the words **OUT** and **NO** two times in the word search below.
The words may go across or down.

D	N	F	N	O	P	O	G
O	B	J	H	C	K	U	N
U	X	N	V	Y	L	T	O
T	A	H	E	Y	J	B	M

Page 125

Sight Word: OUT
Trace the sight word on the dotted lines.
Write it to complete the sentence.

out
OUT

Let's play when we get **out** of school.

| out | out | out |

Color the boxes with the word **out**.

out	our	off
ate	out	too
out	owl	own

311

ANSWER KEY

Page 126

Page 127

Page 128

Page 129

Page 131

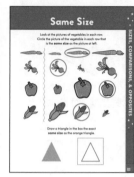

Page 132

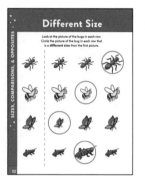

Page 133

Page 134

Page 135

Page 136

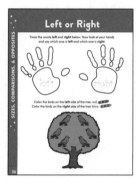

Page 137

Page 138

Page 139

Page 140

Page 141

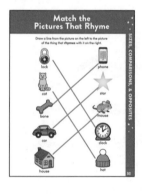

Page 142

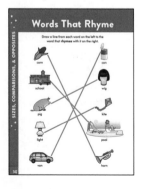

Page 143

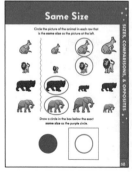

Page 144

Page 145

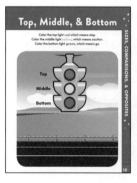

Page 146

ANSWER KEY

Page 147

Page 148

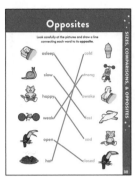

Page 149

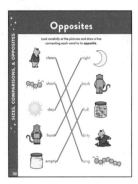

Page 150

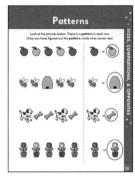

Page 151

Page 152

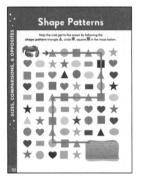

Page 153

Page 154

Page 155

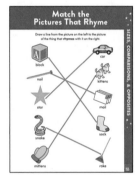

Page 156

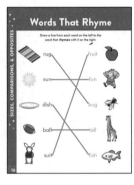

Page 157

Page 158

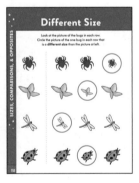

Page 159

Page 160

Page 161

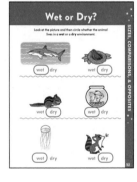

Page 162

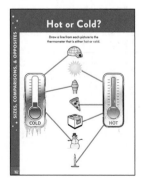

Page 163

Page 164

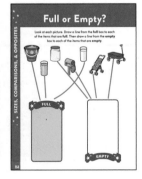

Page 165

Page 166

ANSWER KEY

Page 167

Page 168

Page 169

Page 172

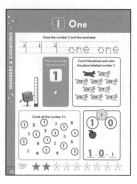

Page 173

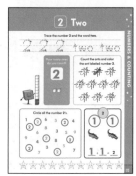

Page 174

Page 175

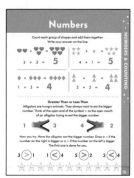

Page 176

Page 177

Page 178

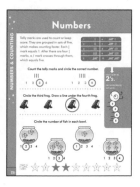

Page 179

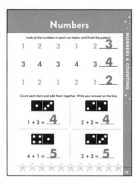

Page 180

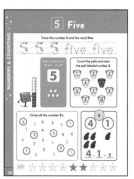

Page 181

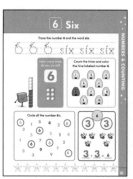

Page 182

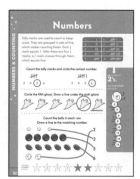

Page 183

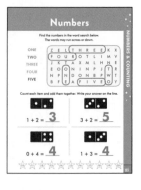

Page 184

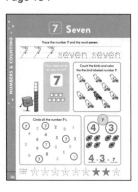

Page 185

Page 186

Page 187

Page 188

ANSWER KEY

Page 189
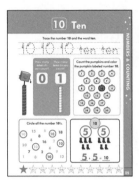

Page 190
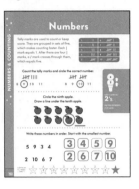

Page 191
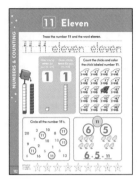

Page 192
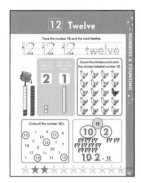

Page 193
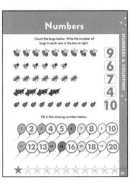

Page 194
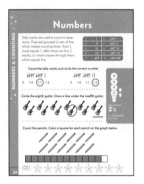

Page 195

Page 196
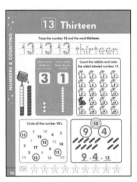

Page 197
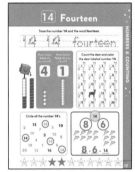

Page 198
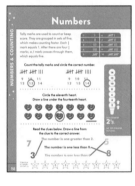

Page 199
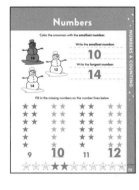

Page 200
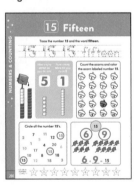

Page 201
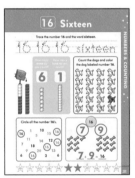

Page 202
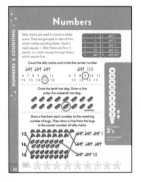

Page 203

Page 204
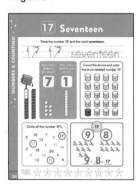

Page 205

Page 206
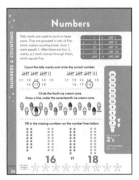

Page 207
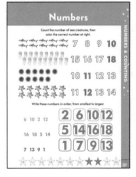

Page 208
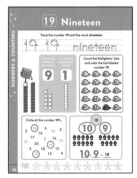

ANSWER KEY

Page 209

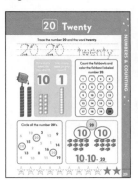

Page 210

Page 211

Page 212

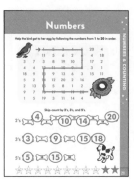

Page 214

Page 215

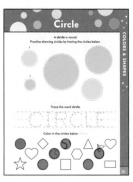

Page 216

Page 217

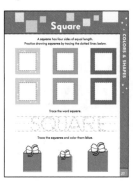

Page 218

Page 220

Page 222

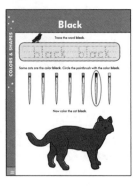

Page 223

Page 224

Page 225

Page 226

Page 227

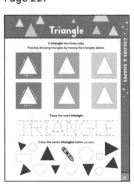

Page 228

Page 229

Page 230

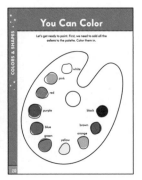

Page 231

ANSWER KEY

Page 232

Missing Colors

Page 233

Find the Cheese

Page 234

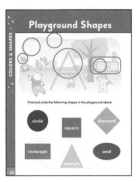

Playground Shapes

Page 235

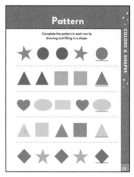

Pattern

Page 236

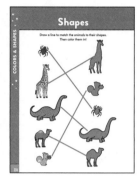

Shapes

Page 238

3-D Shapes

Page 240

Telling Time

Page 241

Telling Time

Page 242

Telling Time

Page 243

What Time Is It?

Page 244

What Time Is It?

Page 245

What Time Is It?

Page 246

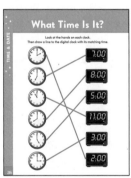

What Time Is It?

Page 247

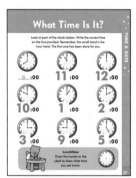

What Time Is It?

Page 248

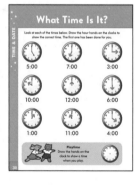

What Time Is It?

Page 250

Days of the Week

Page 251

Days of the Week

Page 252

Months of the Year

Page 254

Months of the Year

Page 255

Fourth of July

ANSWER KEY

Page 256

Halloween

Page 259

Valentine's Day

Page 265

My Birthday

Page 266

Morning and Night Routine

Page 267

Exercise Is Fun!

Page 268

Hand Washing

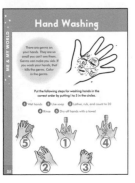

Page 269

Your Teeth

Page 270

Tying Your Shoes

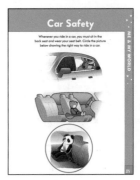

Page 275

Car Safety

Page 276

Helmets

Page 277

Crossing the Street

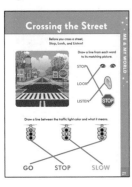

Page 278

Places in My Neighborhood

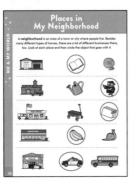

Page 279

People in My Neighborhood

Page 281

Animals and Their Babies

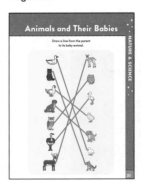

Page 282

What Is Making That Noise?

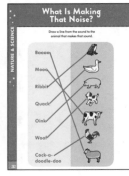

Page 283

House, Farm, or Zoo?

Page 284

Animal Word Search

Page 285

Feather, Fur, or Scales

Page 286

Animal Habitats: Forest

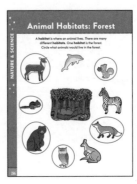

Page 287

Animal Habitats: Savanna